Carol Hopkins

Coloring for All Ages

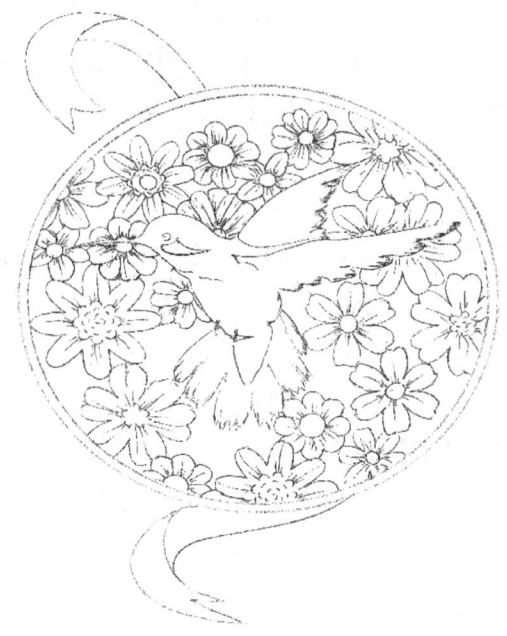

by

Carol Hopkins

Shywind Creations, Carol Hopkins
carol@shywindcreations.com

Ordering Information:
Quantity sales. Special discounts are available on quantity purchases by corporations, associations, and others. For details, contact the publisher at the address above. Printed in the United States of America.

Butterflies 35 drawings

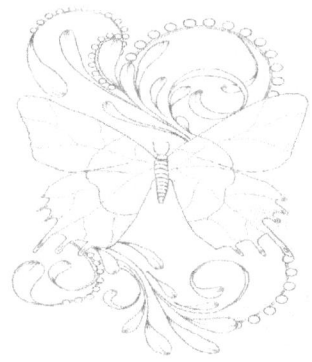

Relaxation 40 drawings

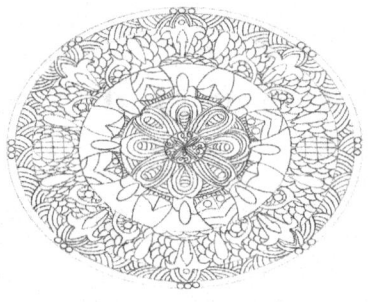

Masks 30 drawings

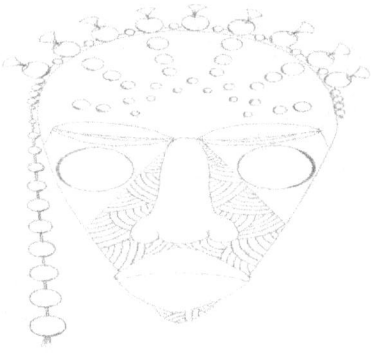

DEDICATION

To those who want to add color to their lives.

To all the nurses who work in our senior facilities.

ACKNOWLEDGMENTS

My husband is the greatest supporter for any project I decide to do.

Thank you, my love, for your help.

There is an artist in everyone.

INTRODUCTION

Coloring for All Ages by Carol Hopkins offers 100+ stress relief patterns on one-sided pages. Carol has combined her three popular coloring books into one: Butterflies, Masks, and Relaxation patterns. Use your choice of markers, fine tip pens, colored pencils, or crayons. Coloring is known to be therapeutic for all ages, so detach yourself with many assorted designs to choose from.

Coloring for All Ages will bring hours of stress relief, an alternative to meditation, relieve tension and anxiety, and provide hours of relaxation for the whole family.

I designed my coloring books for every age. My drawings are all hand drawn to bring the artist out in you. Color and frame your masterpiece to hang on your wall or give as a gift of love.

Butterflies

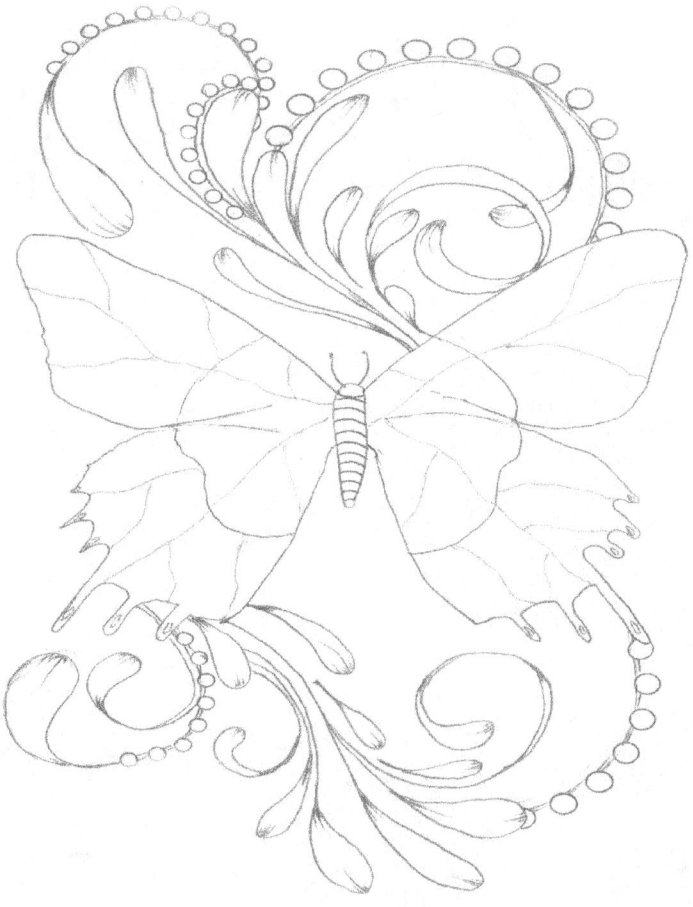

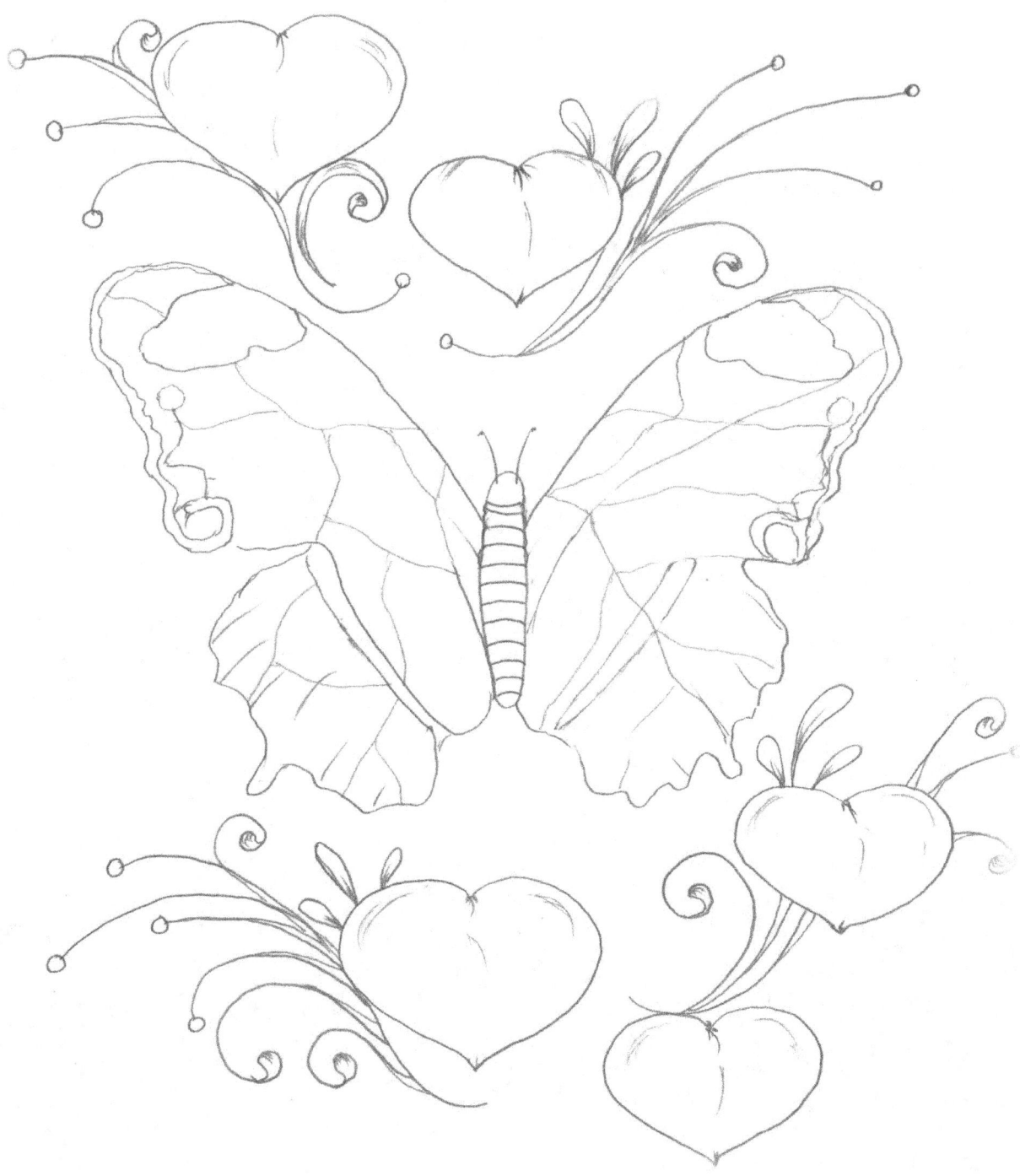

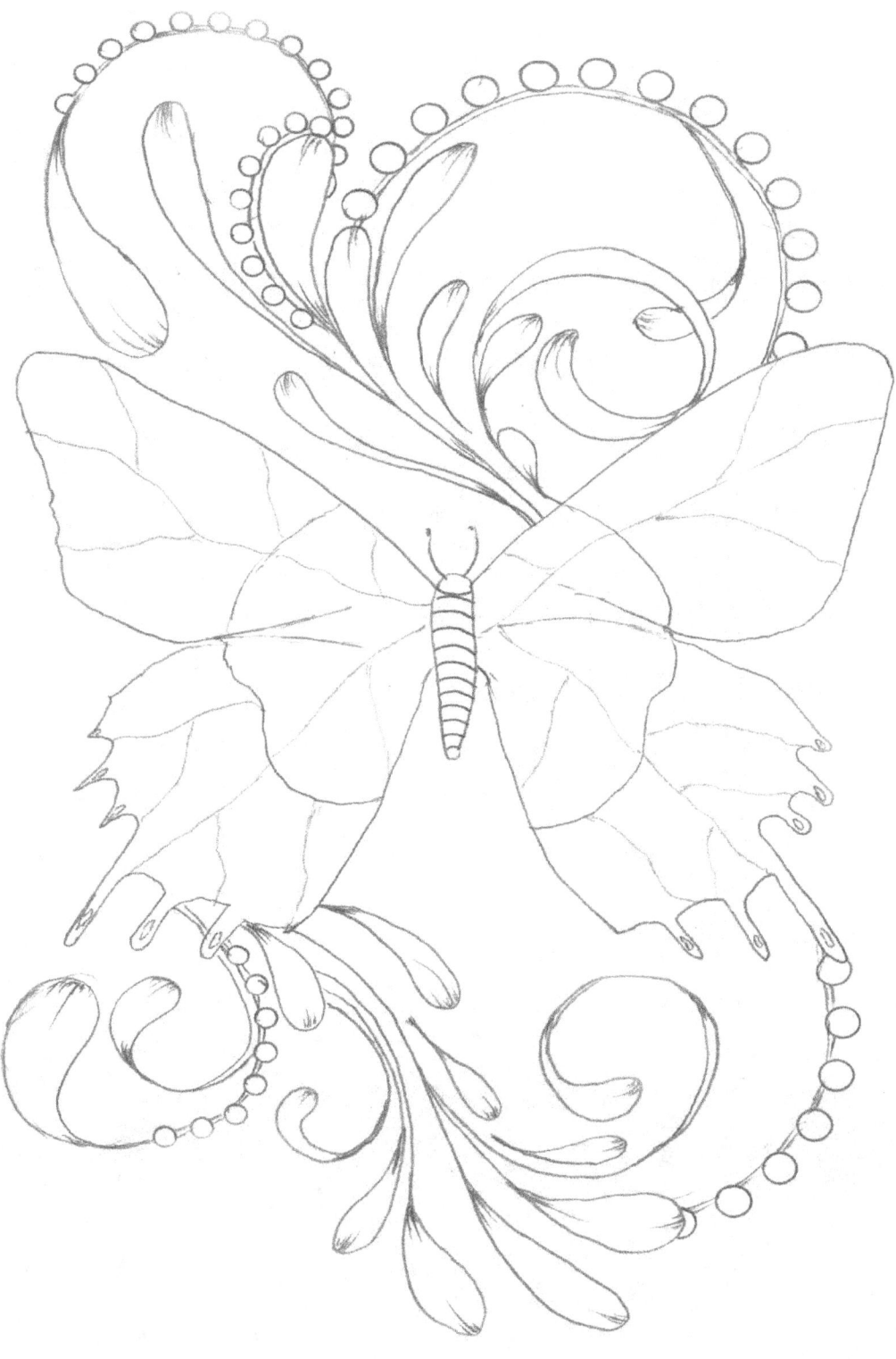

Carol Hopkins

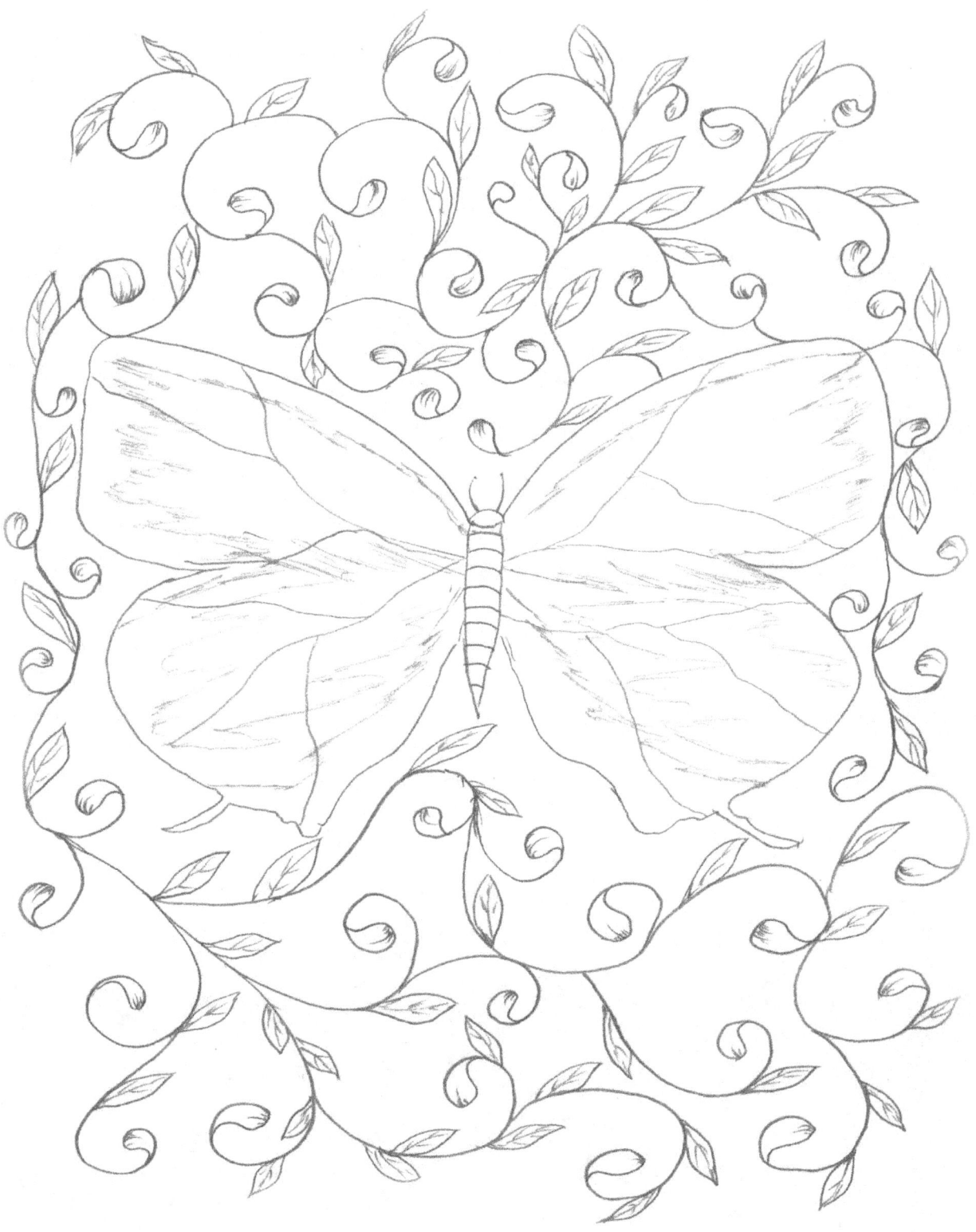

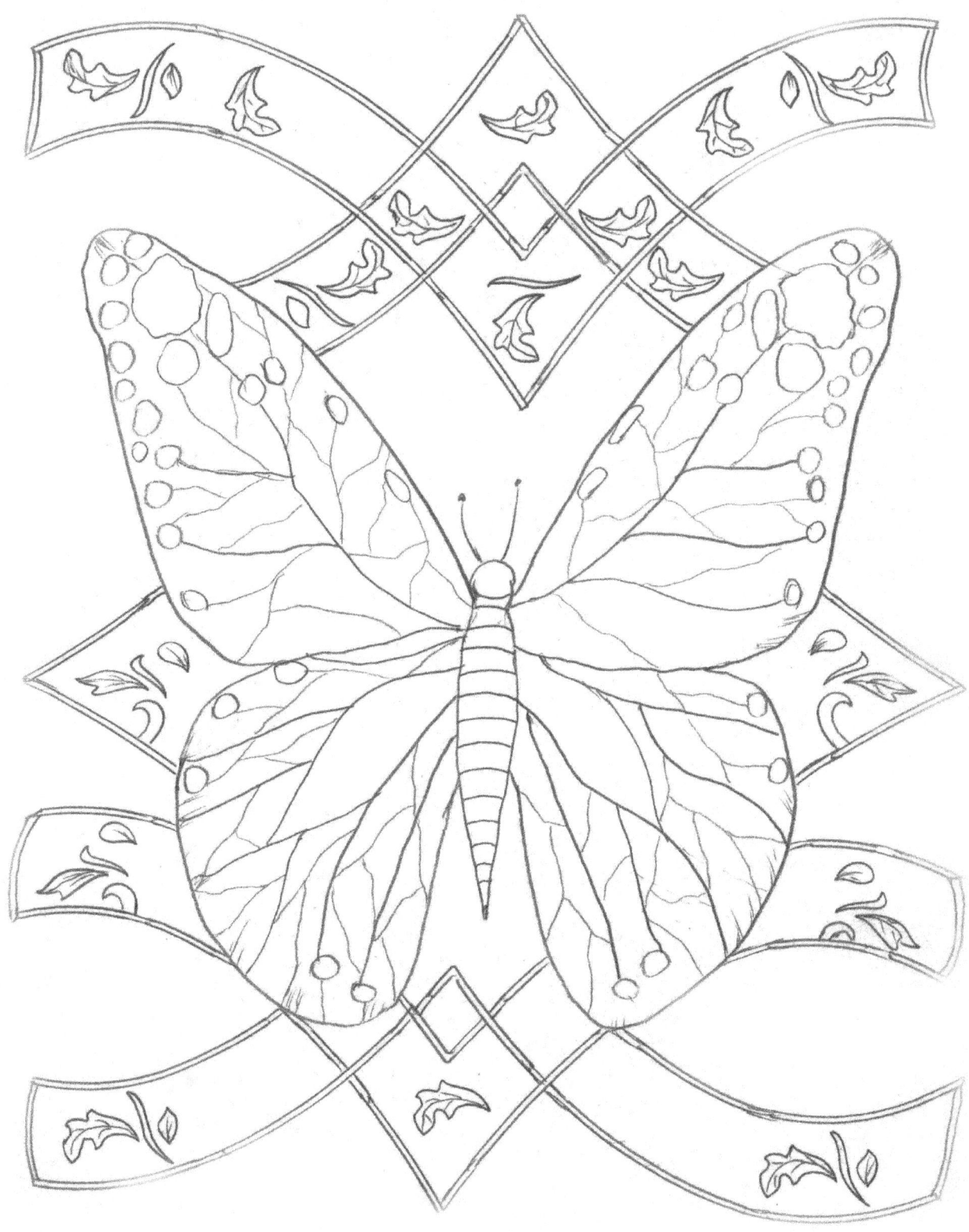

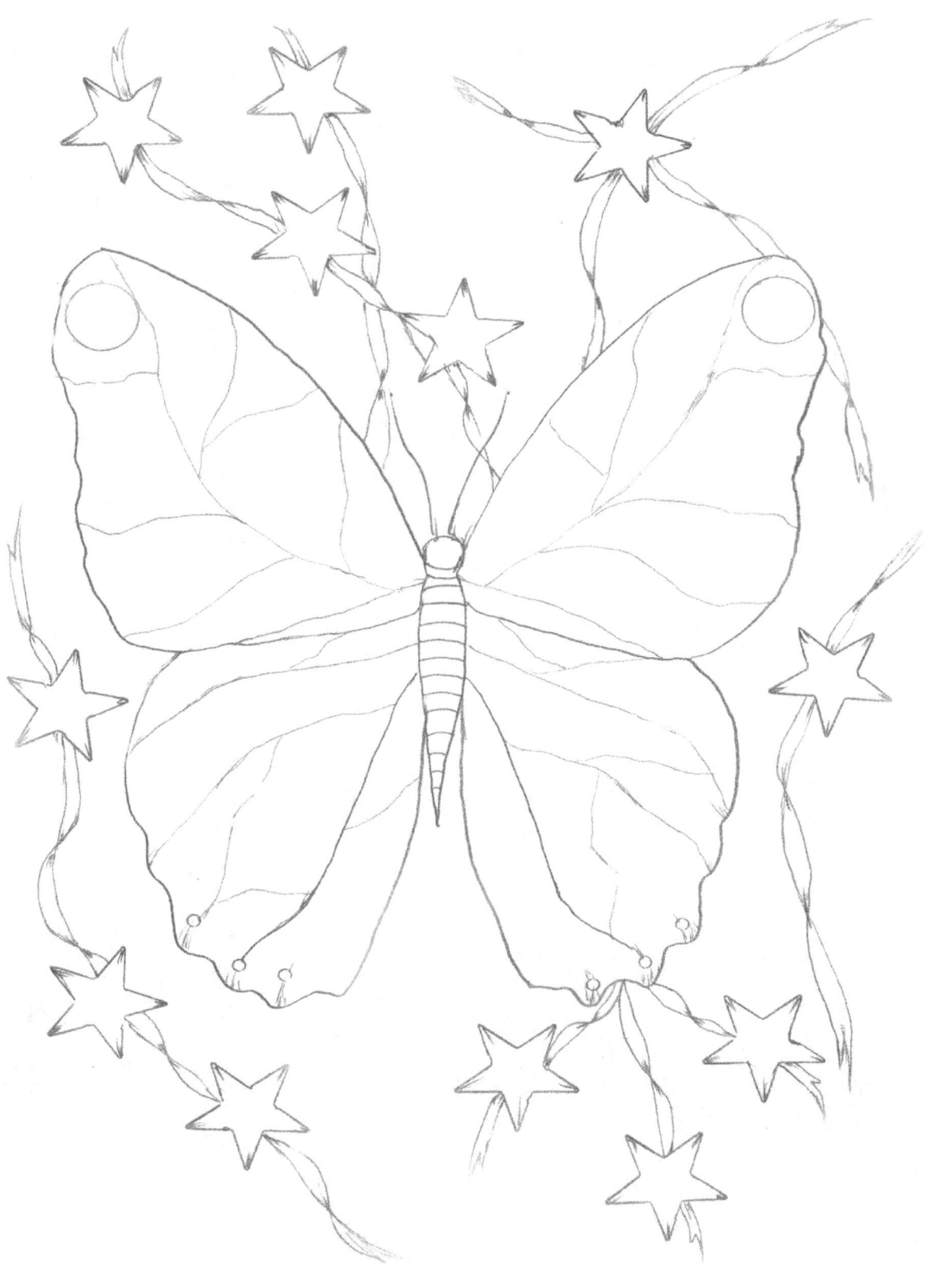

Carol Hopkins

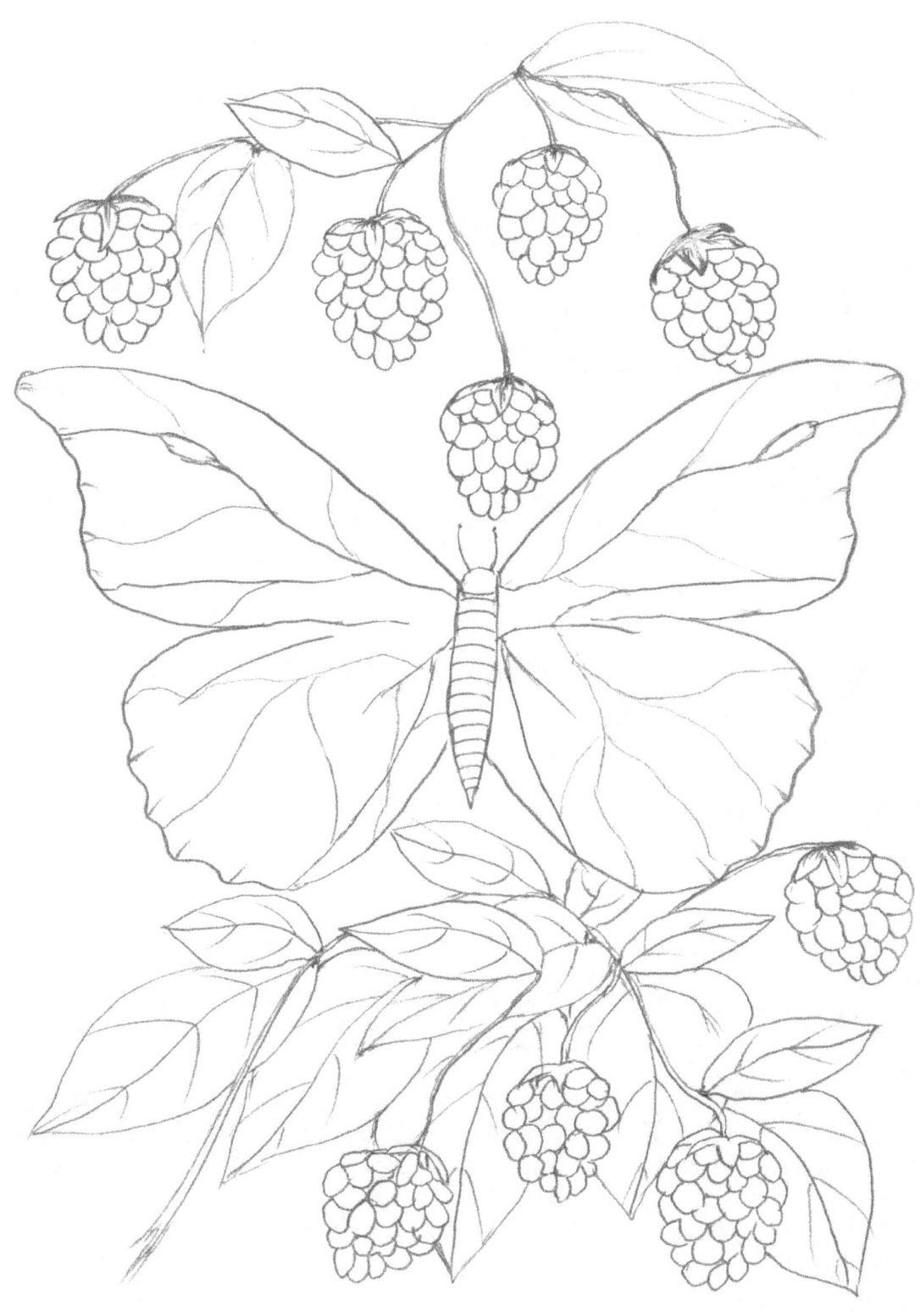

Carol Hopkins

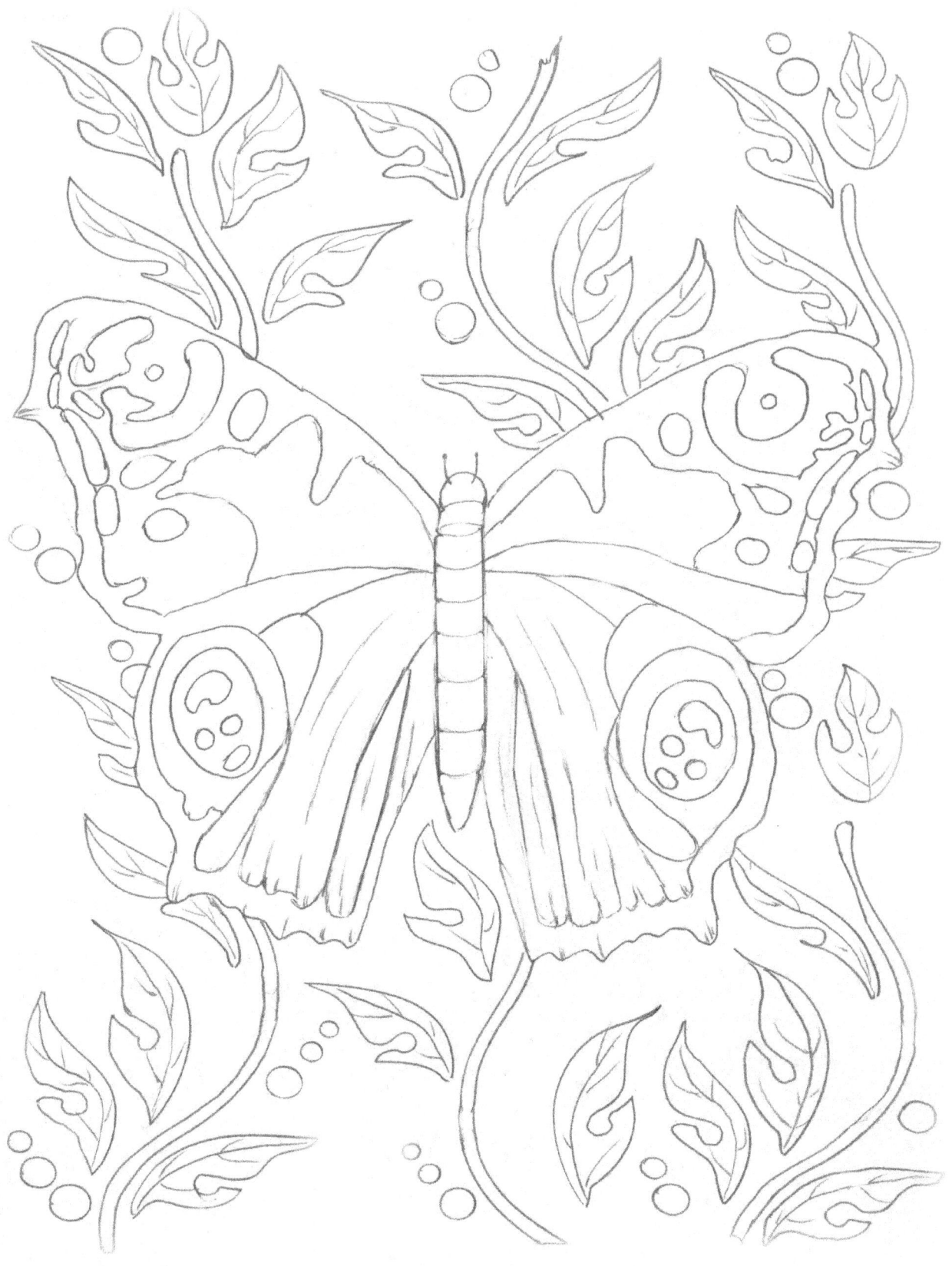

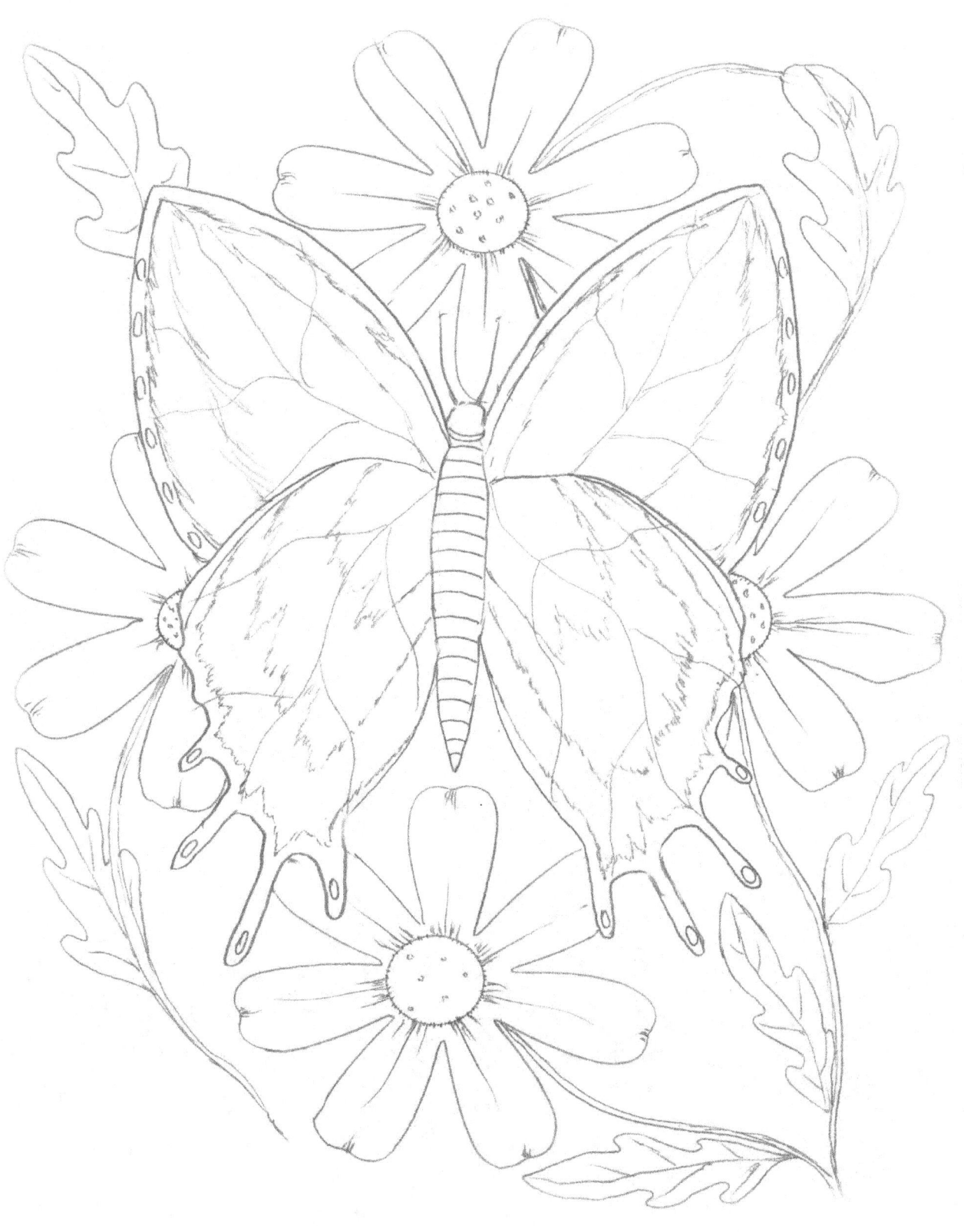

Carol Hopkins

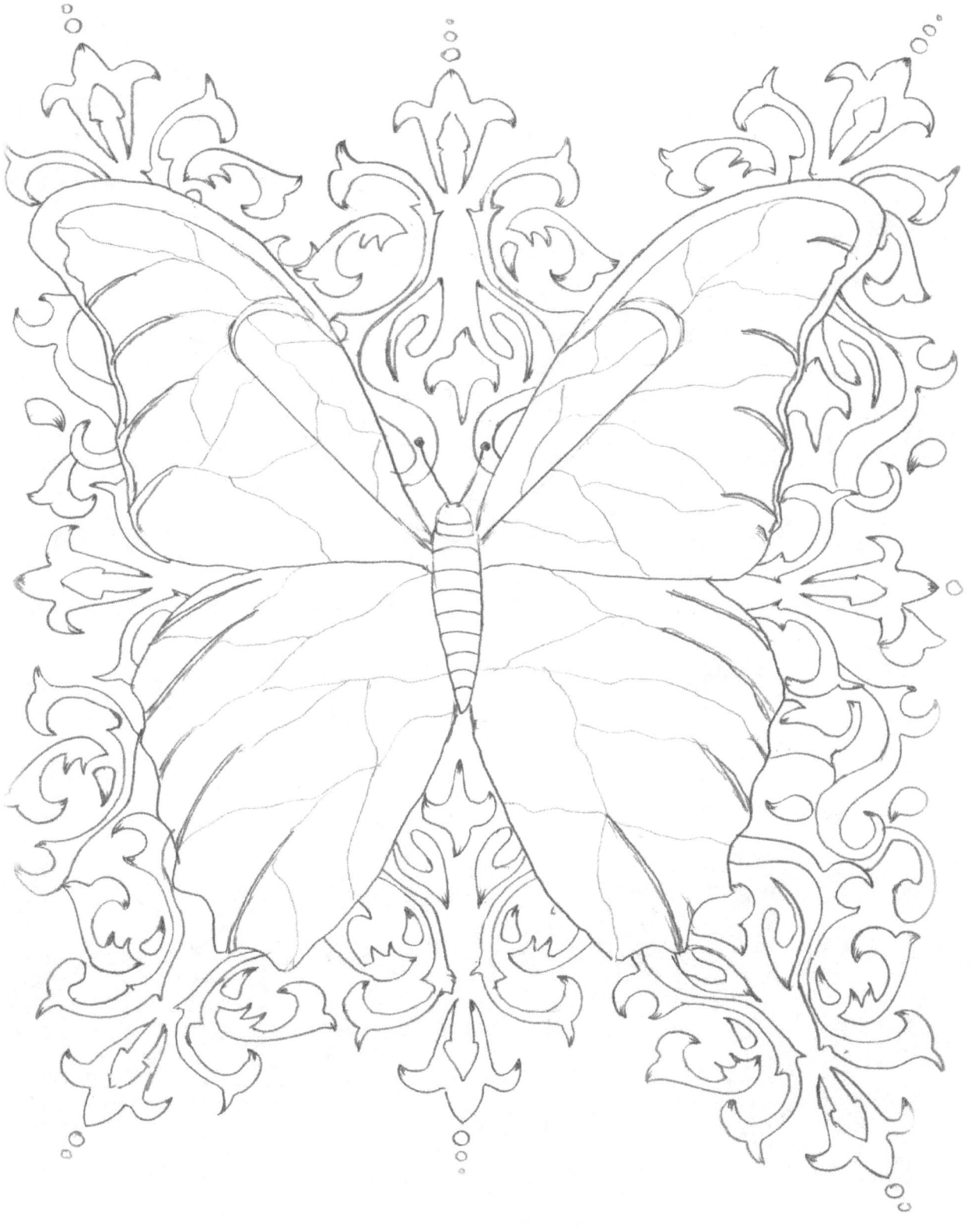

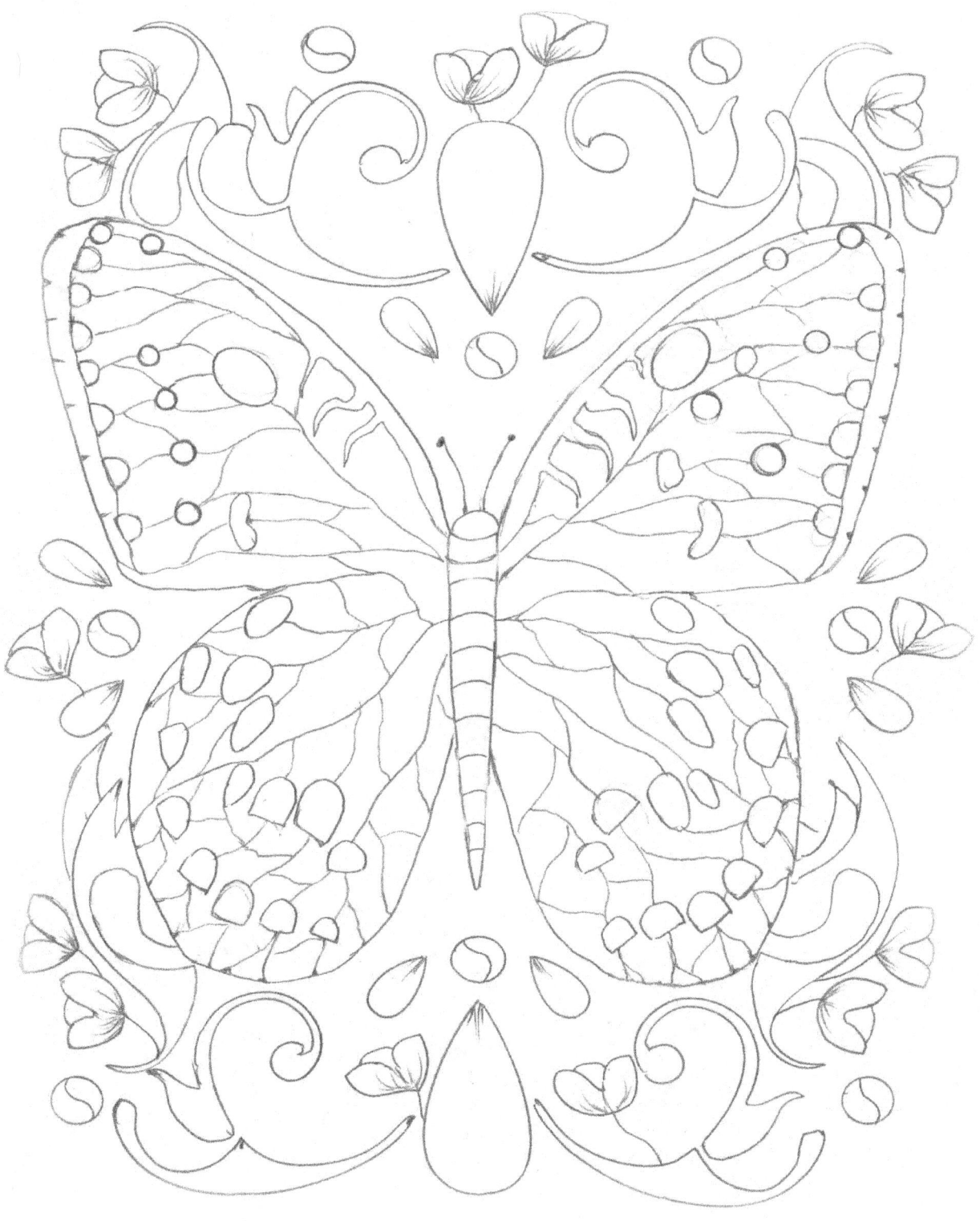

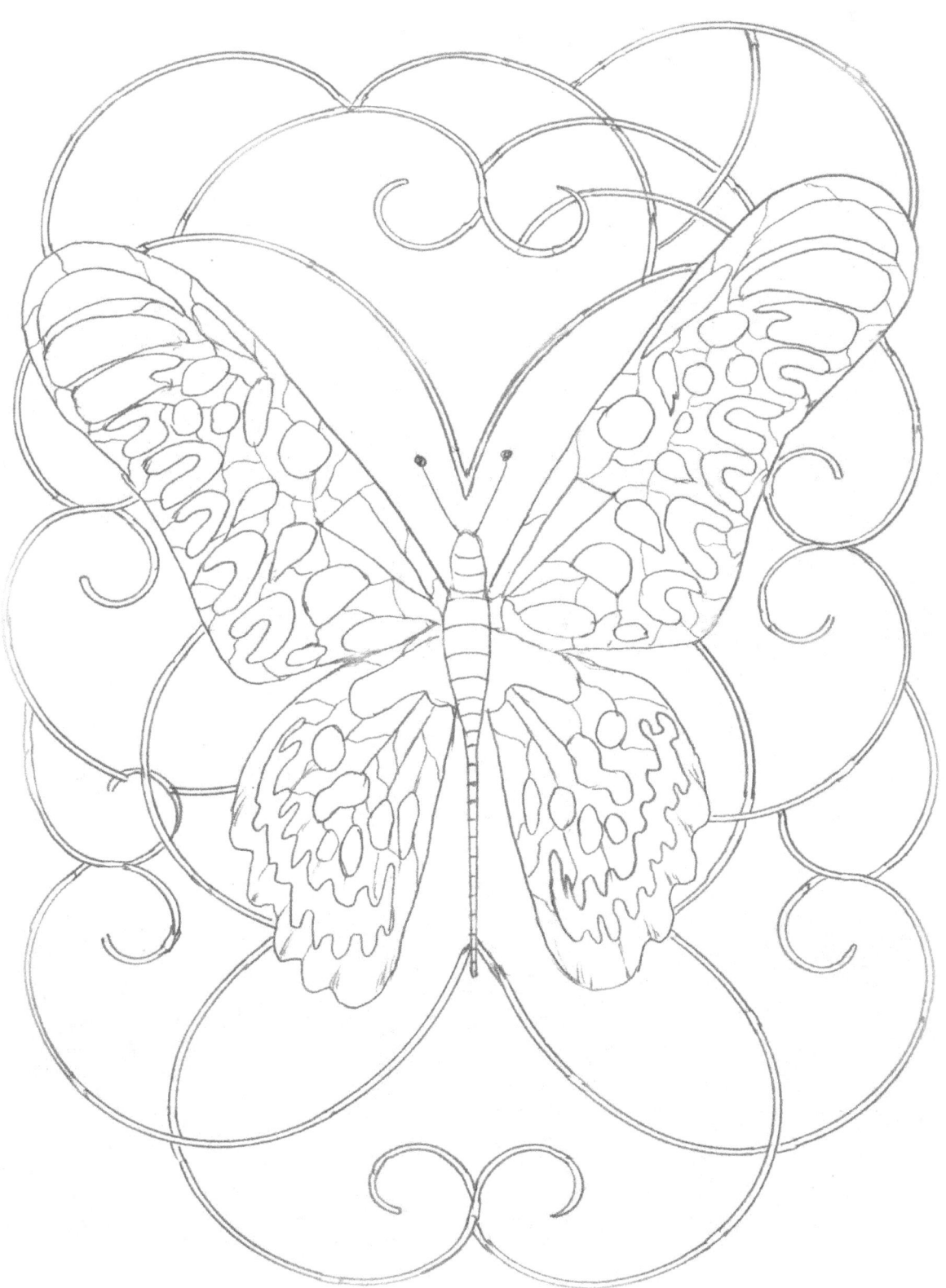

Carol Hopkins

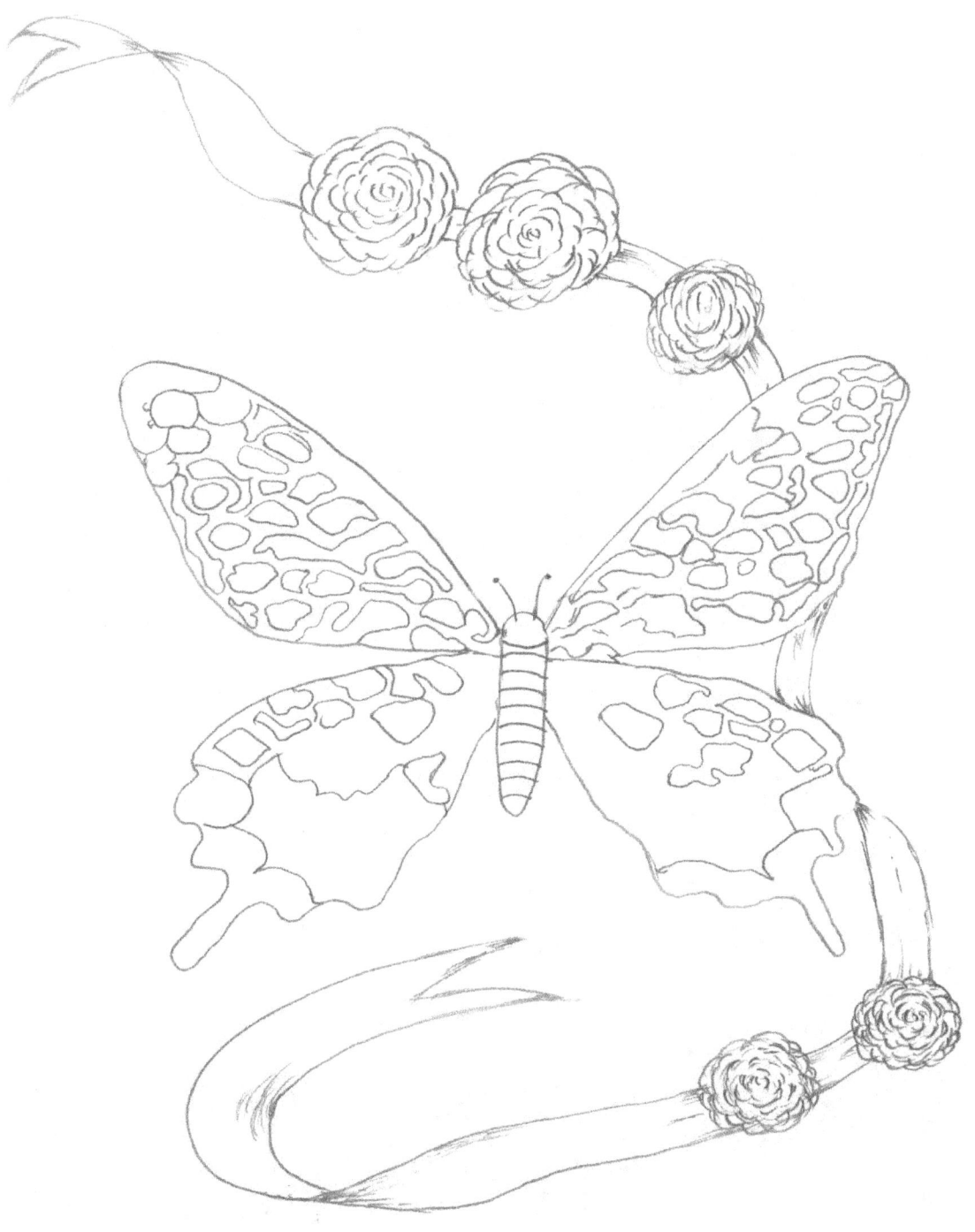

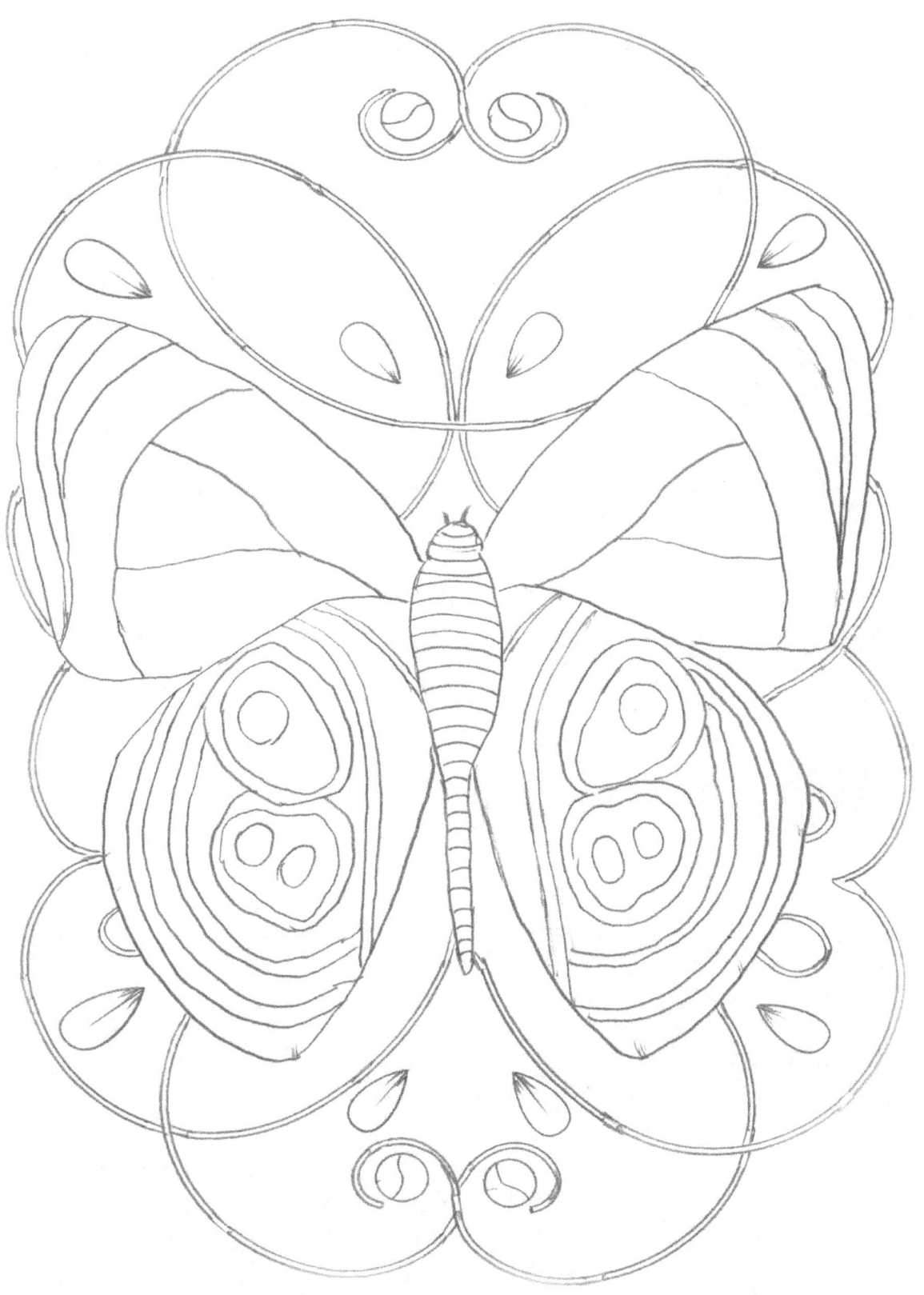

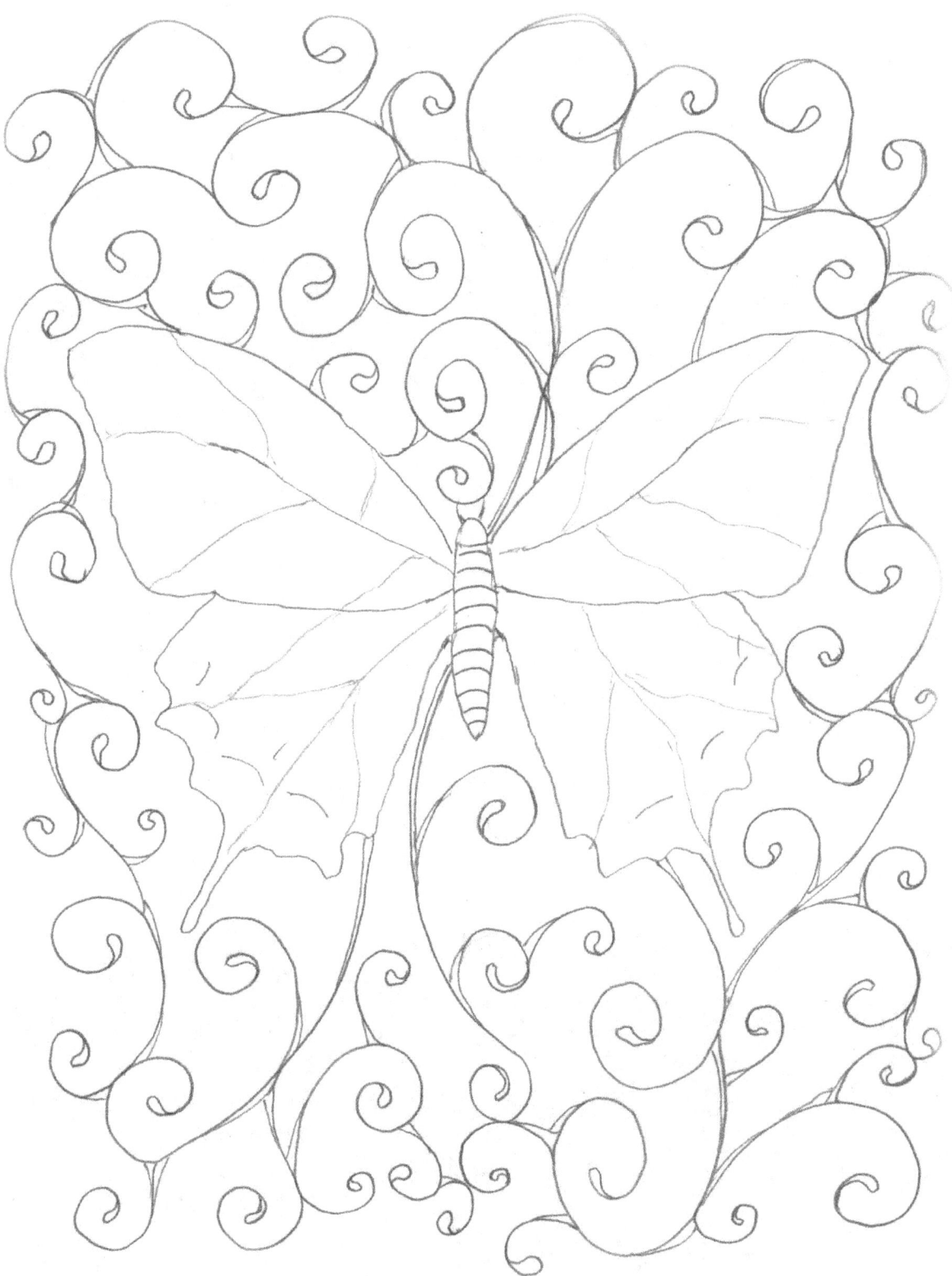

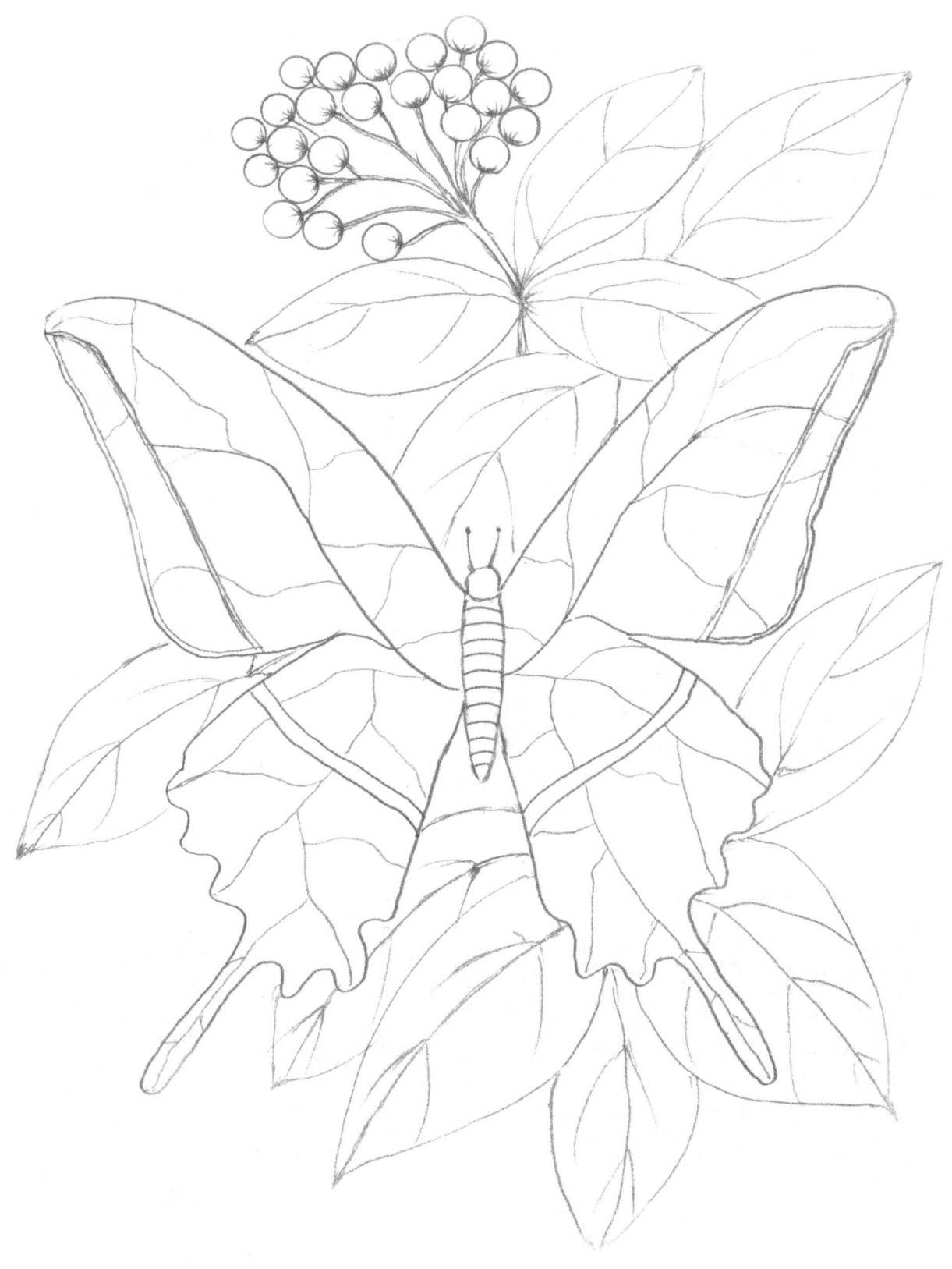

Carol Hopkins

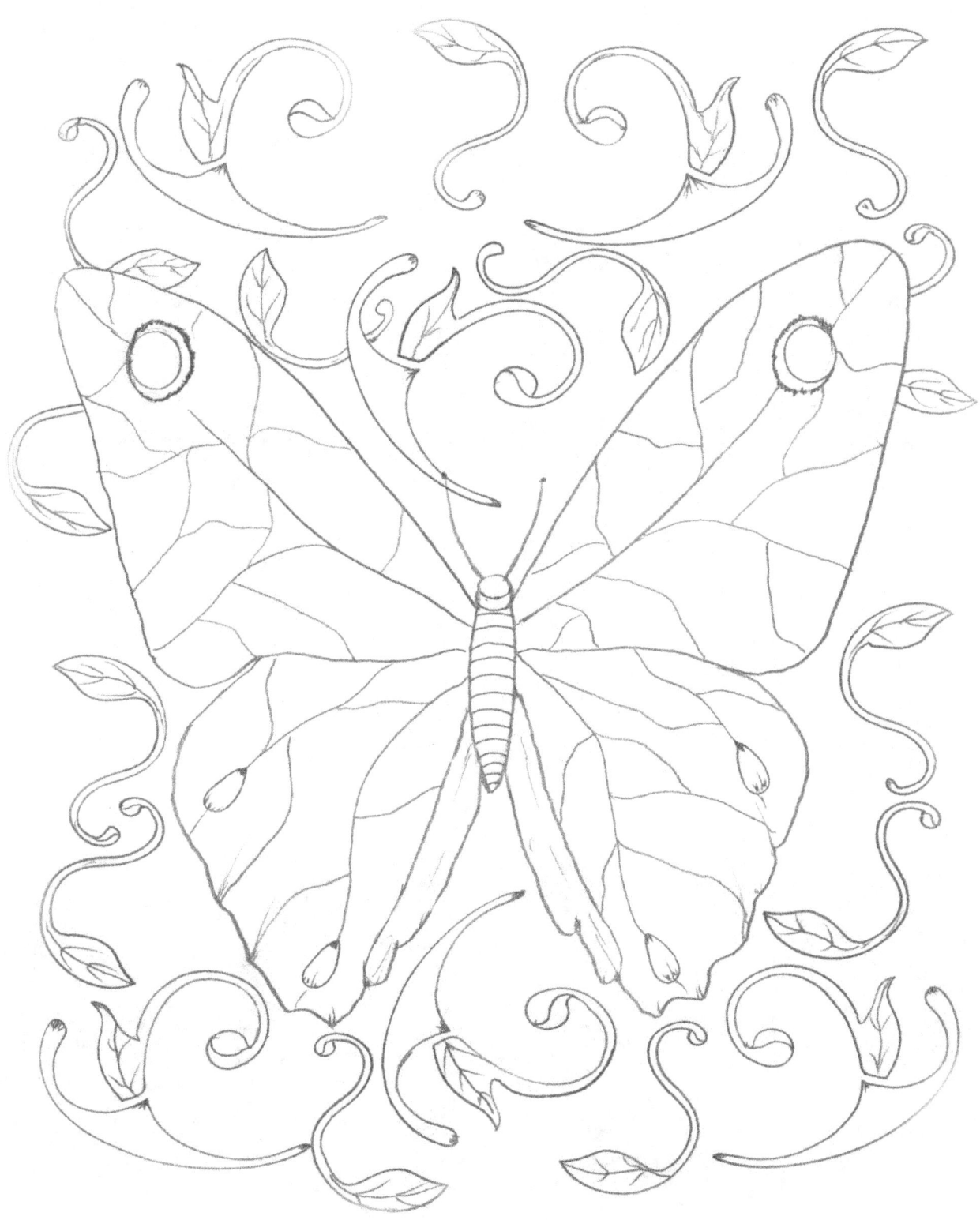

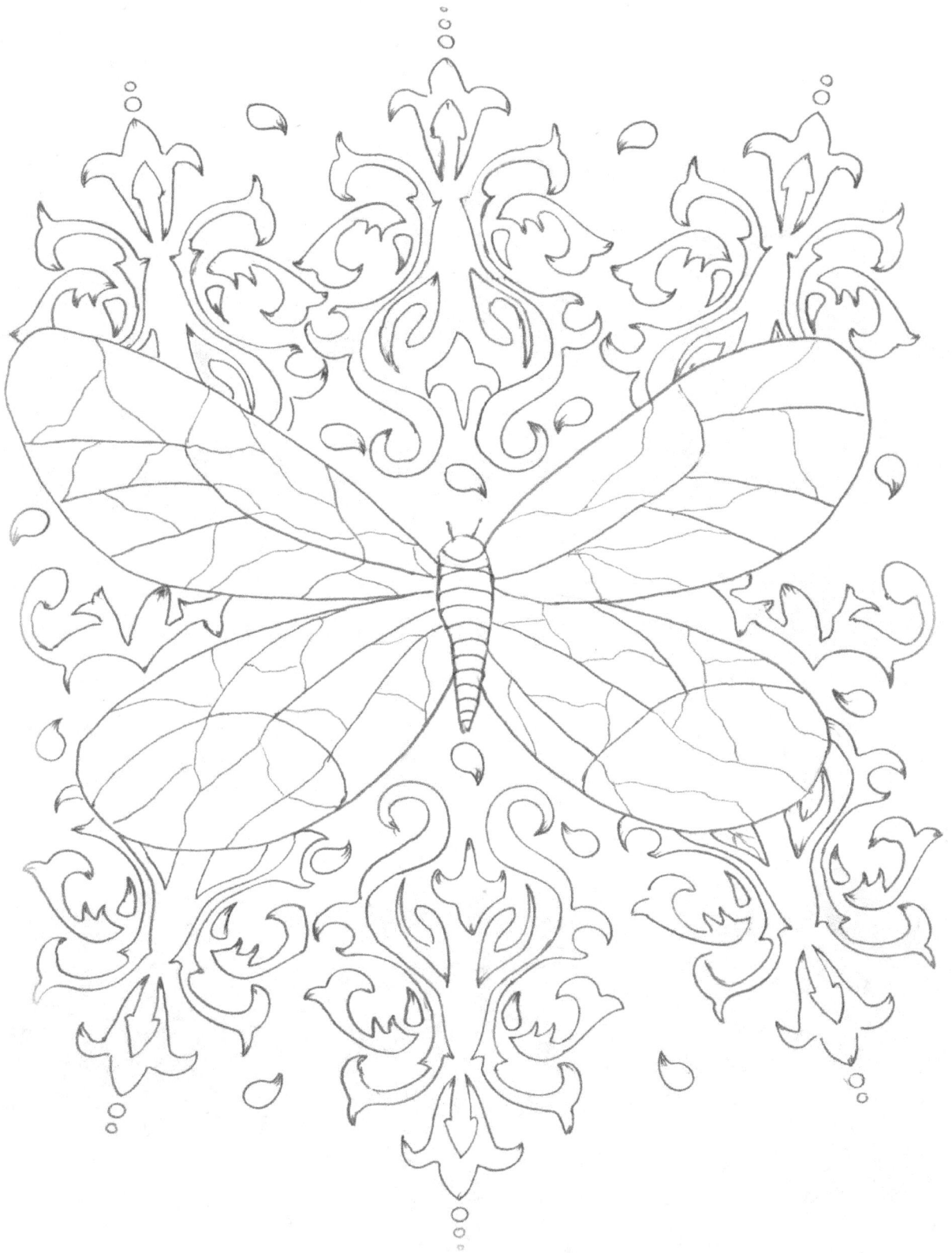

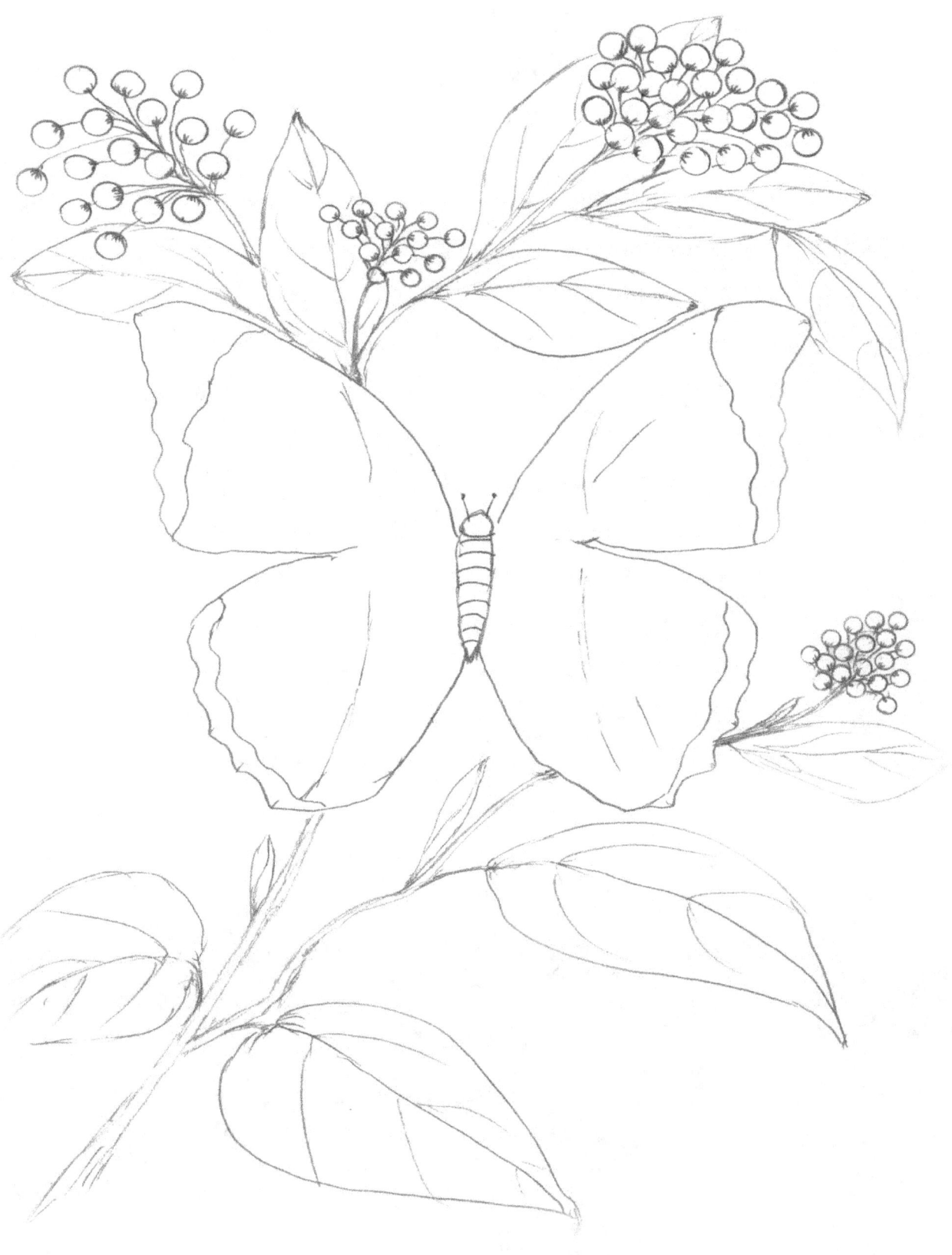

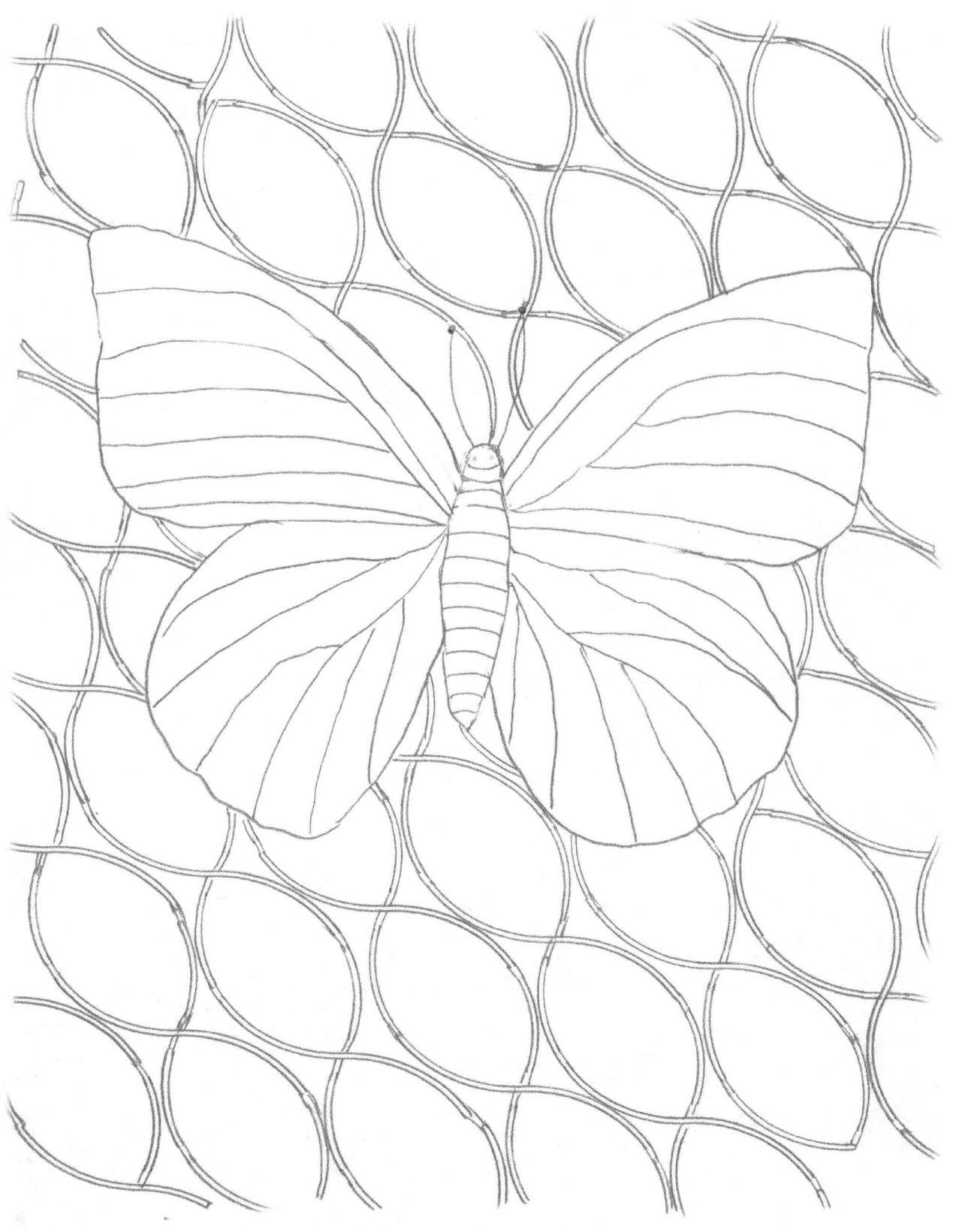

Carol Hopkins

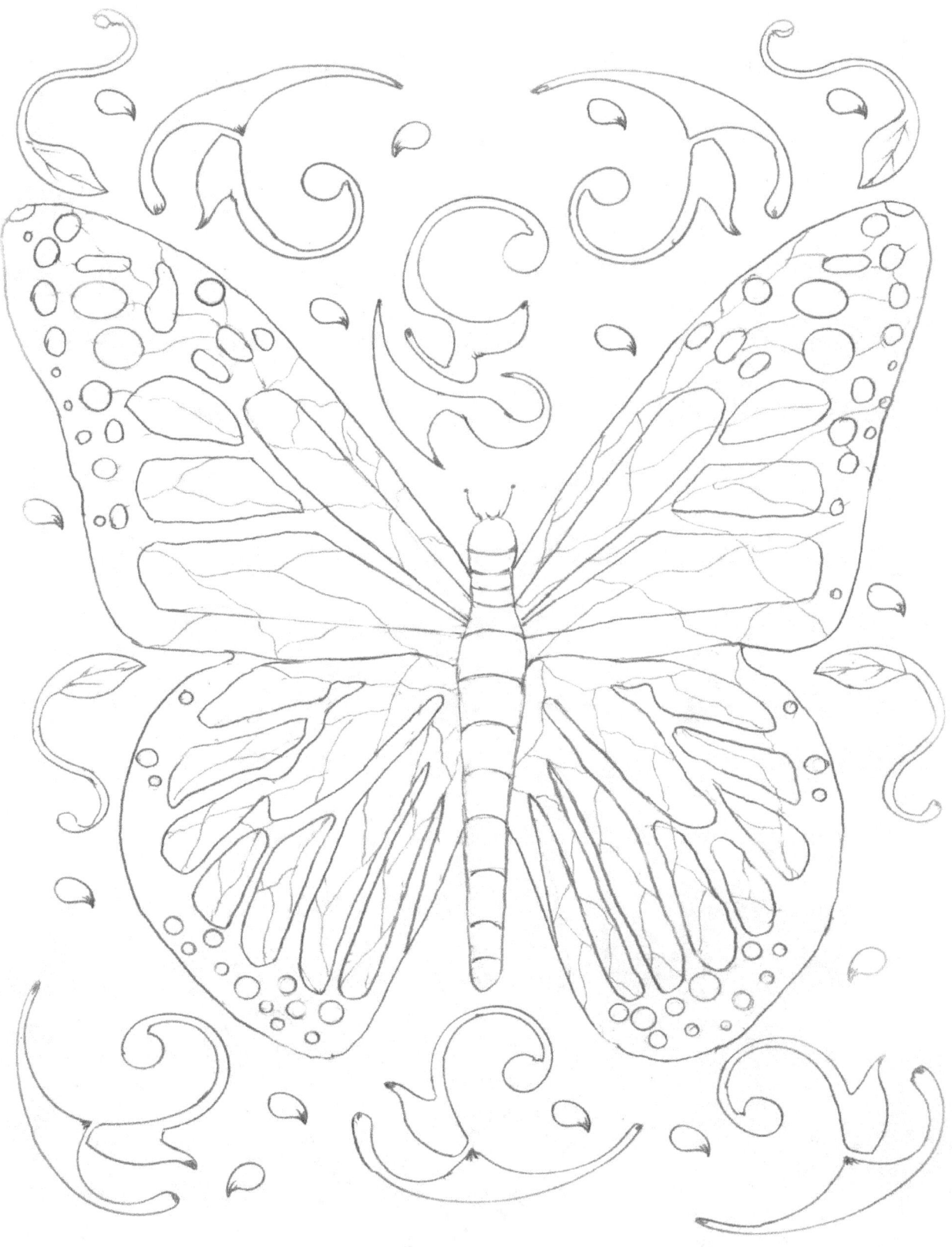

Carol Hopkins

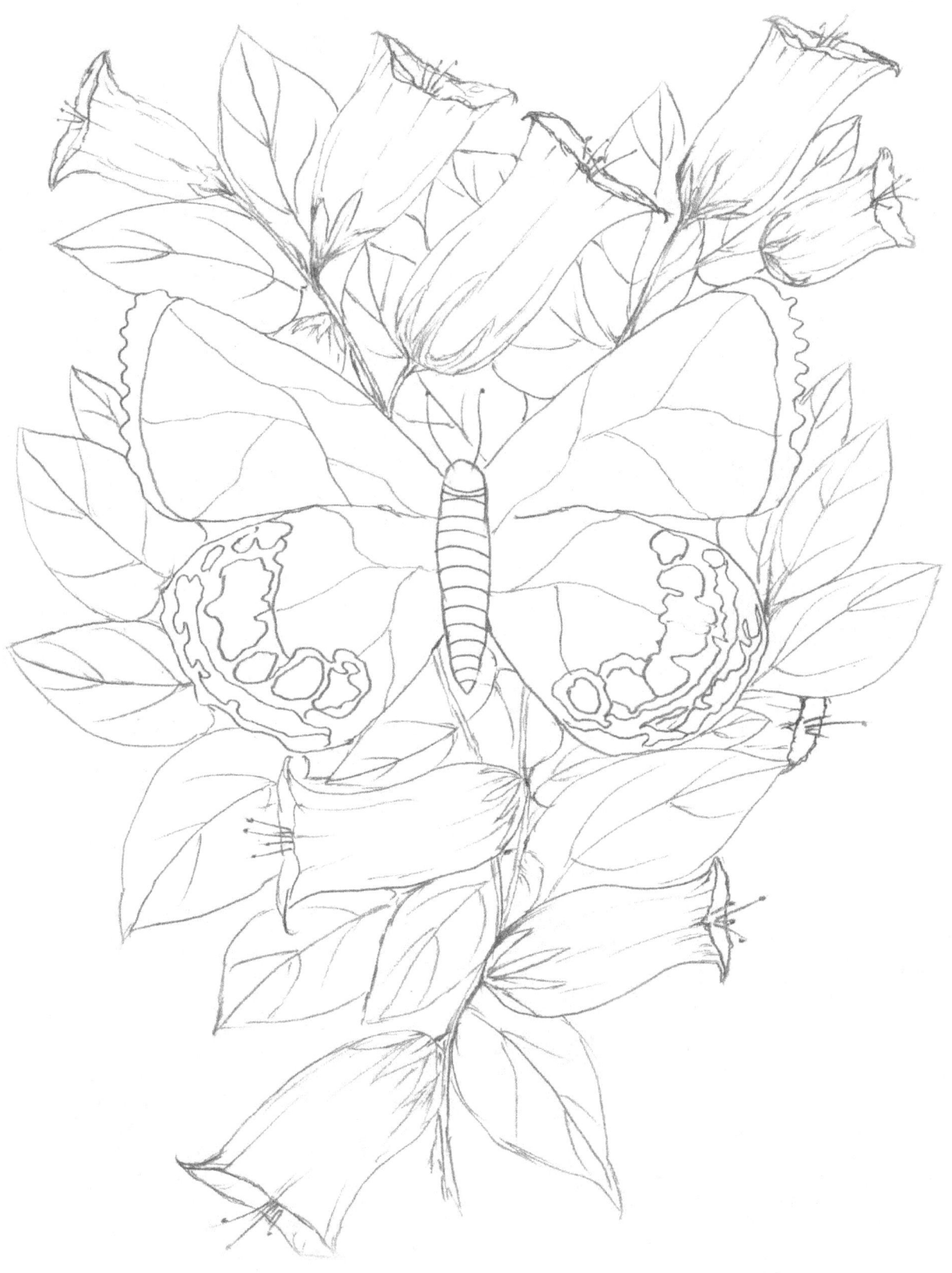

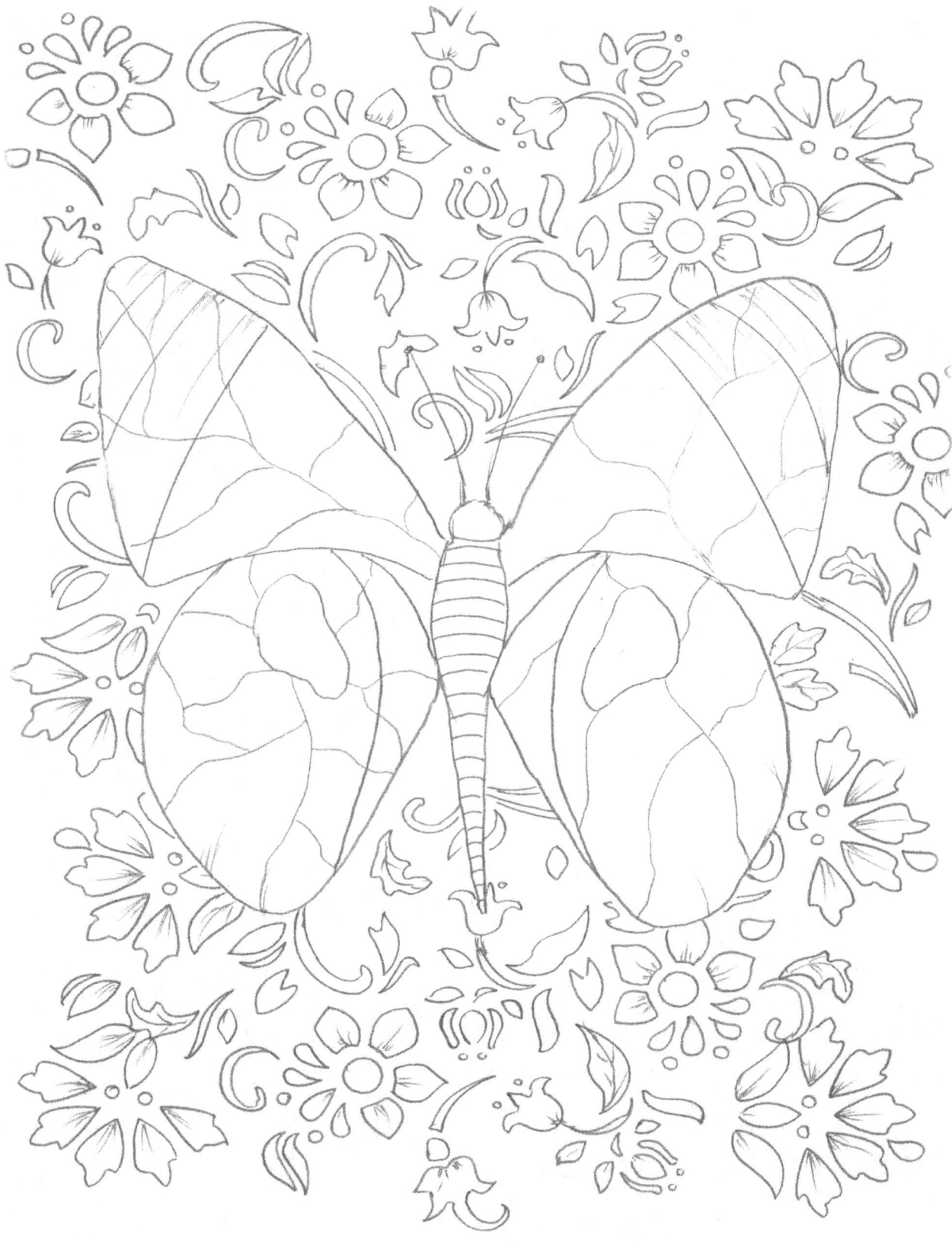

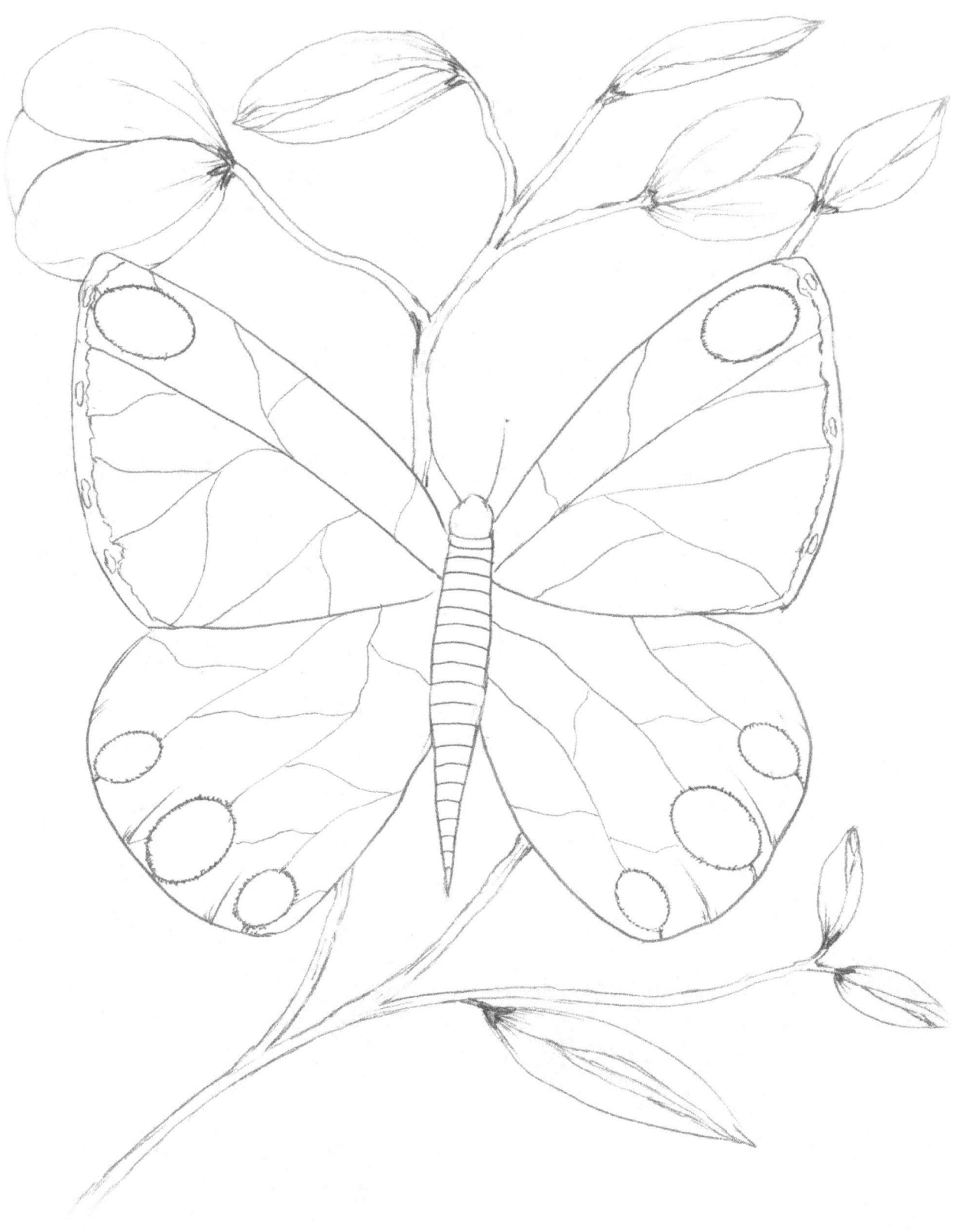

Carol Hopkins

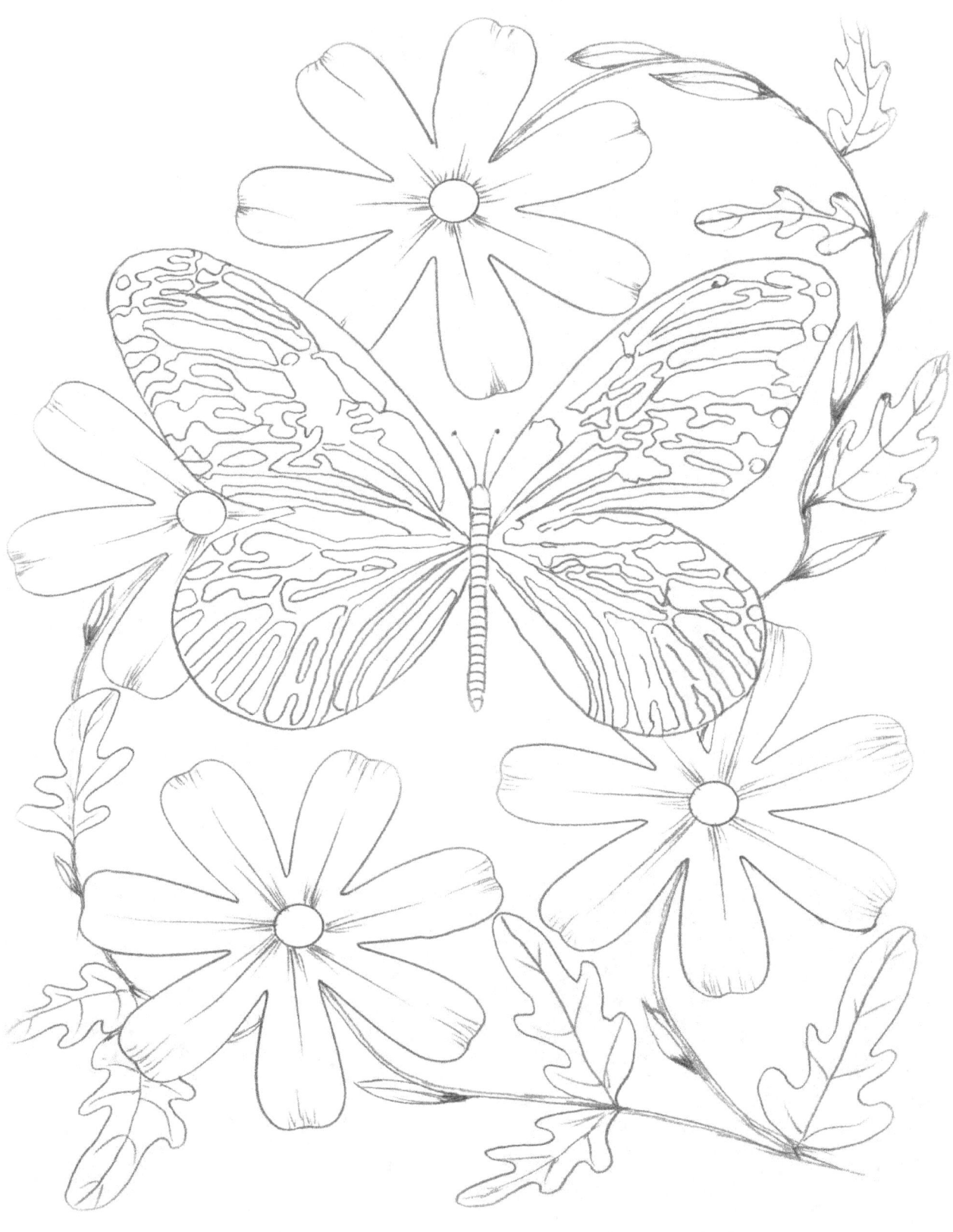

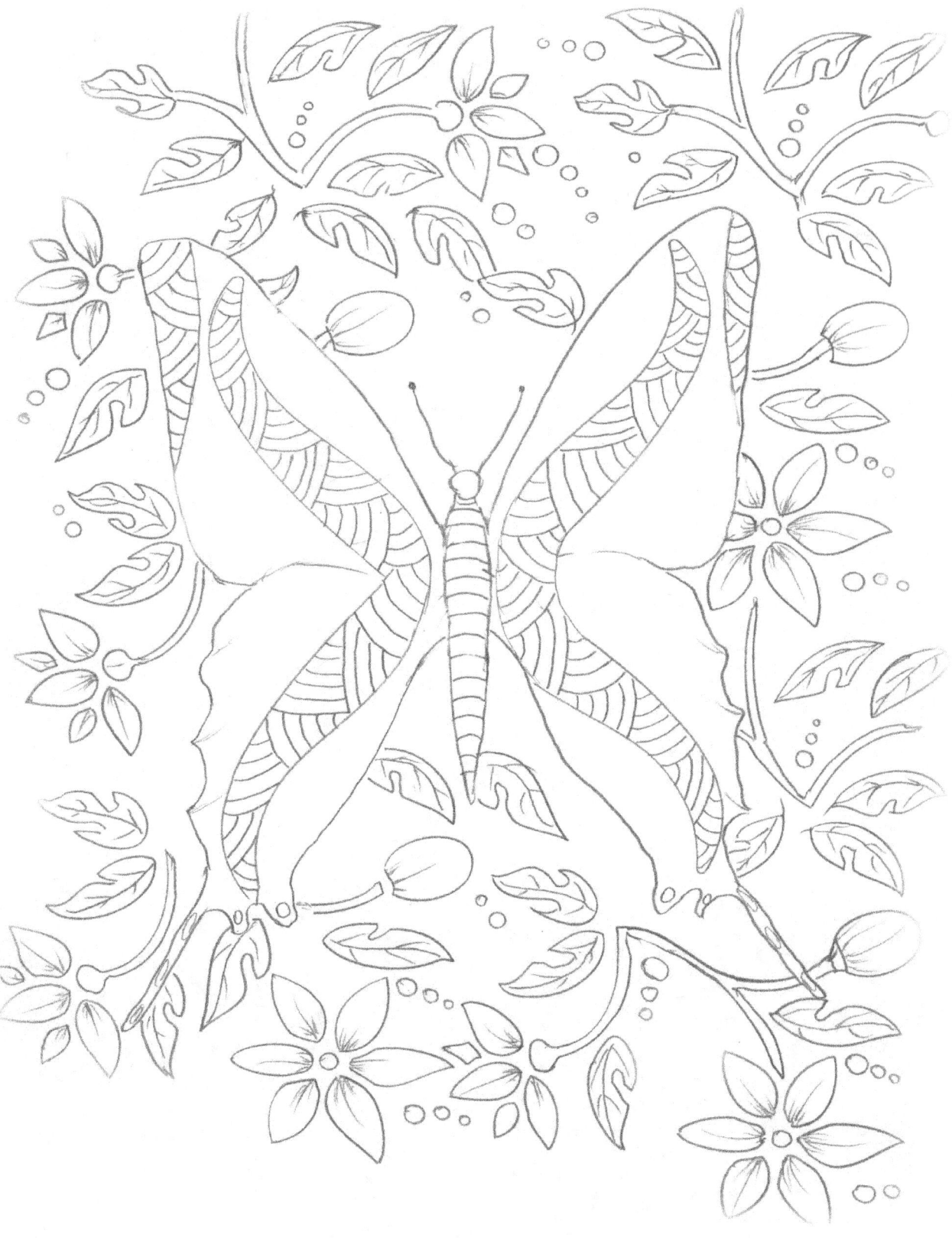

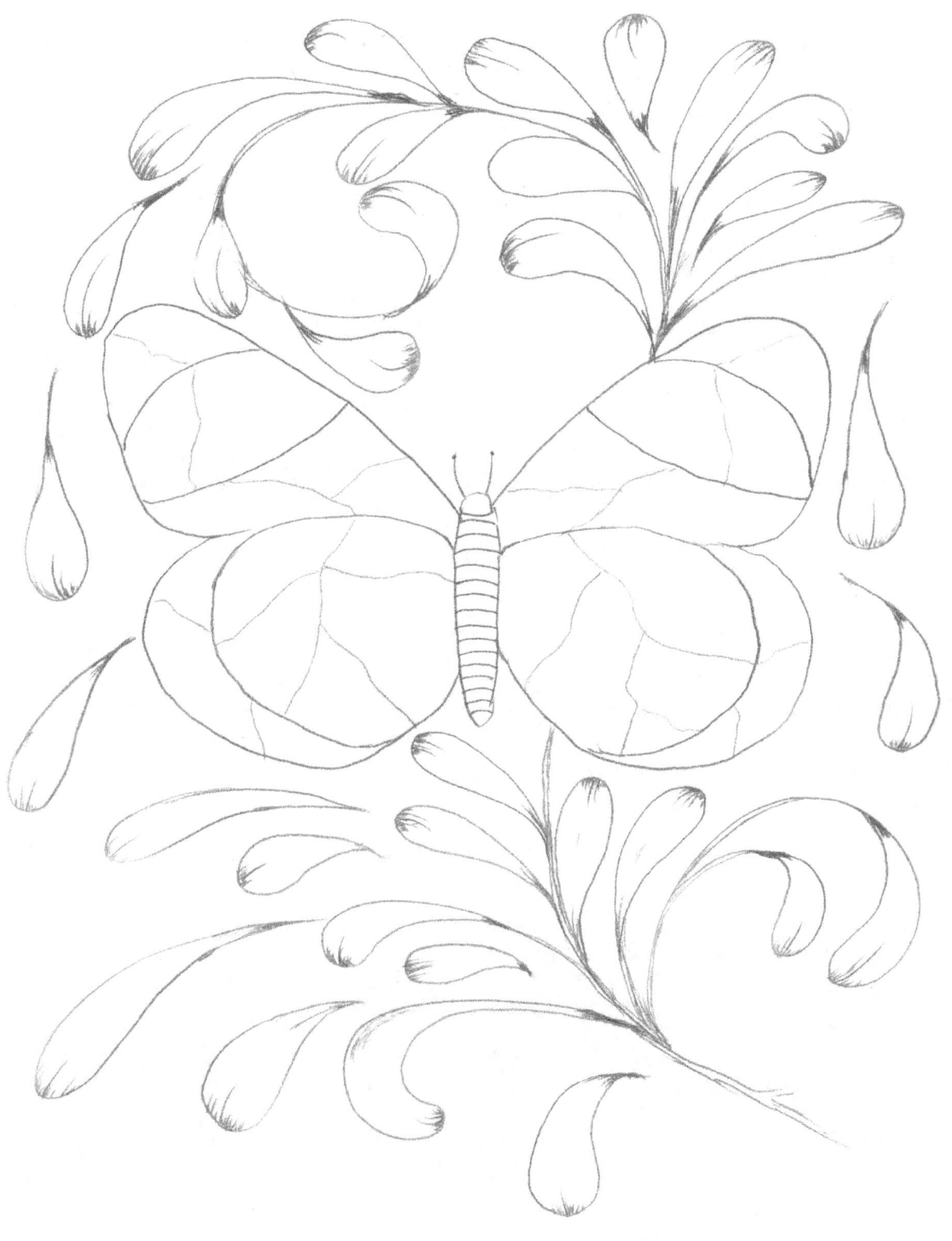

Carol Hopkins

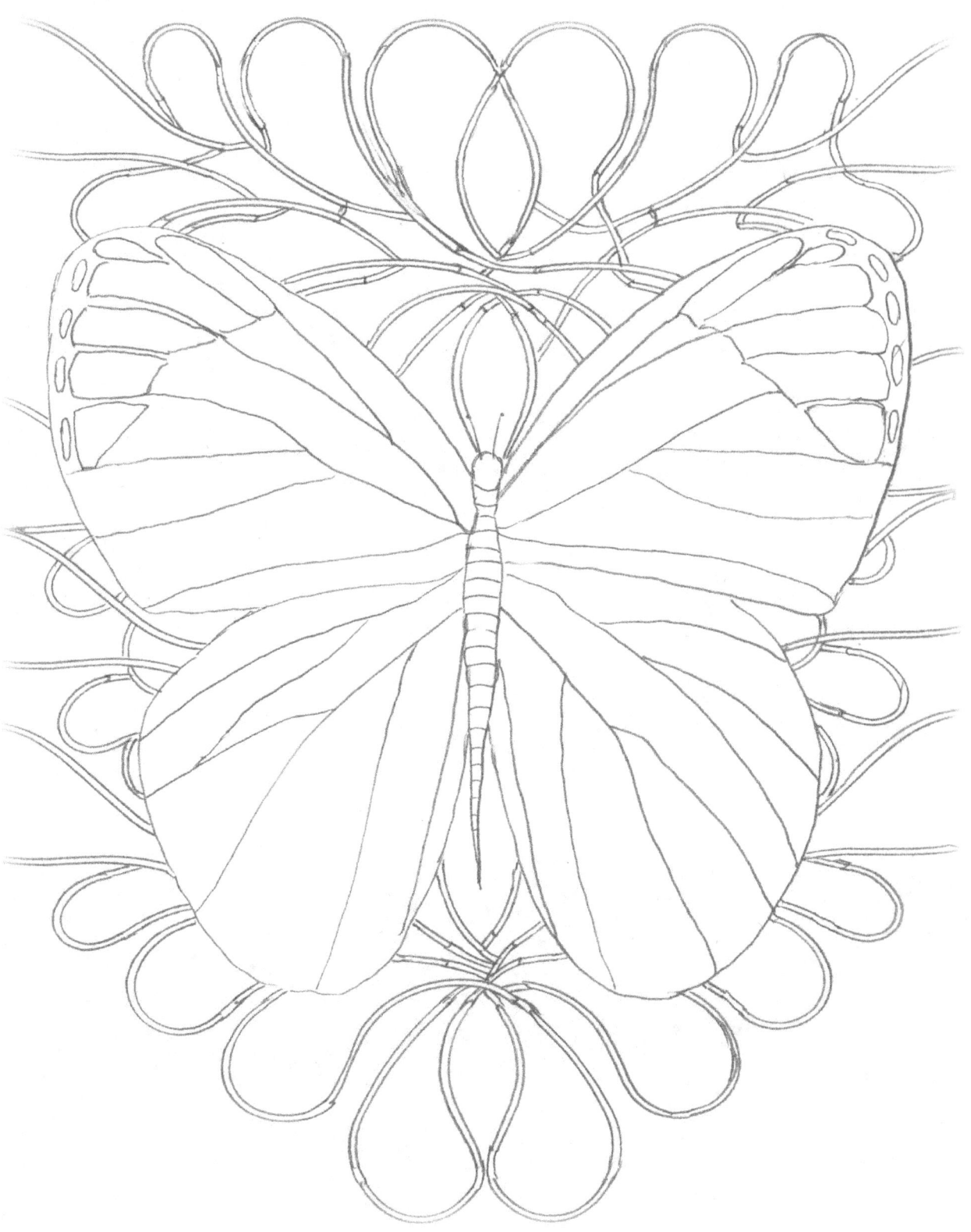

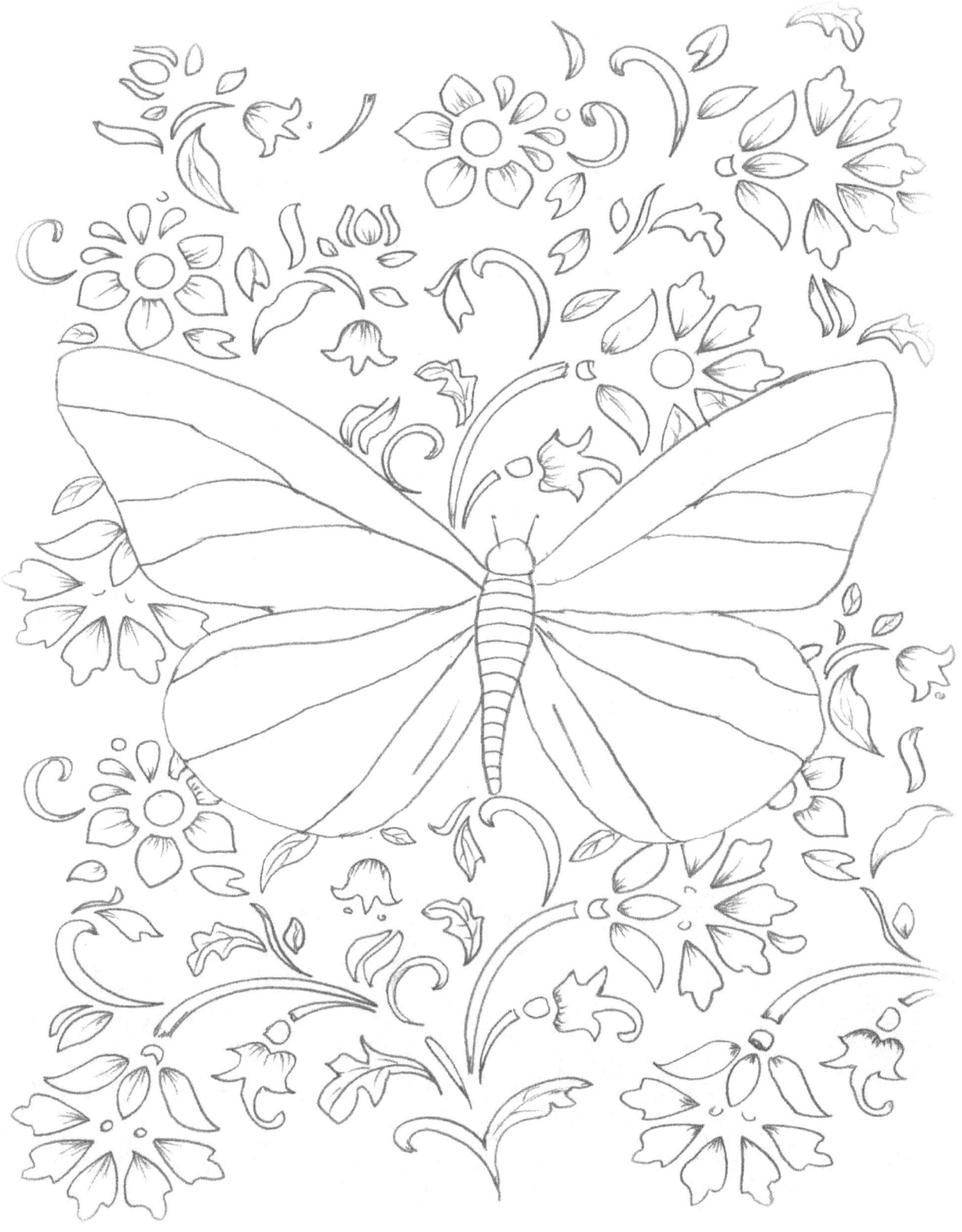

Carol Hopkins

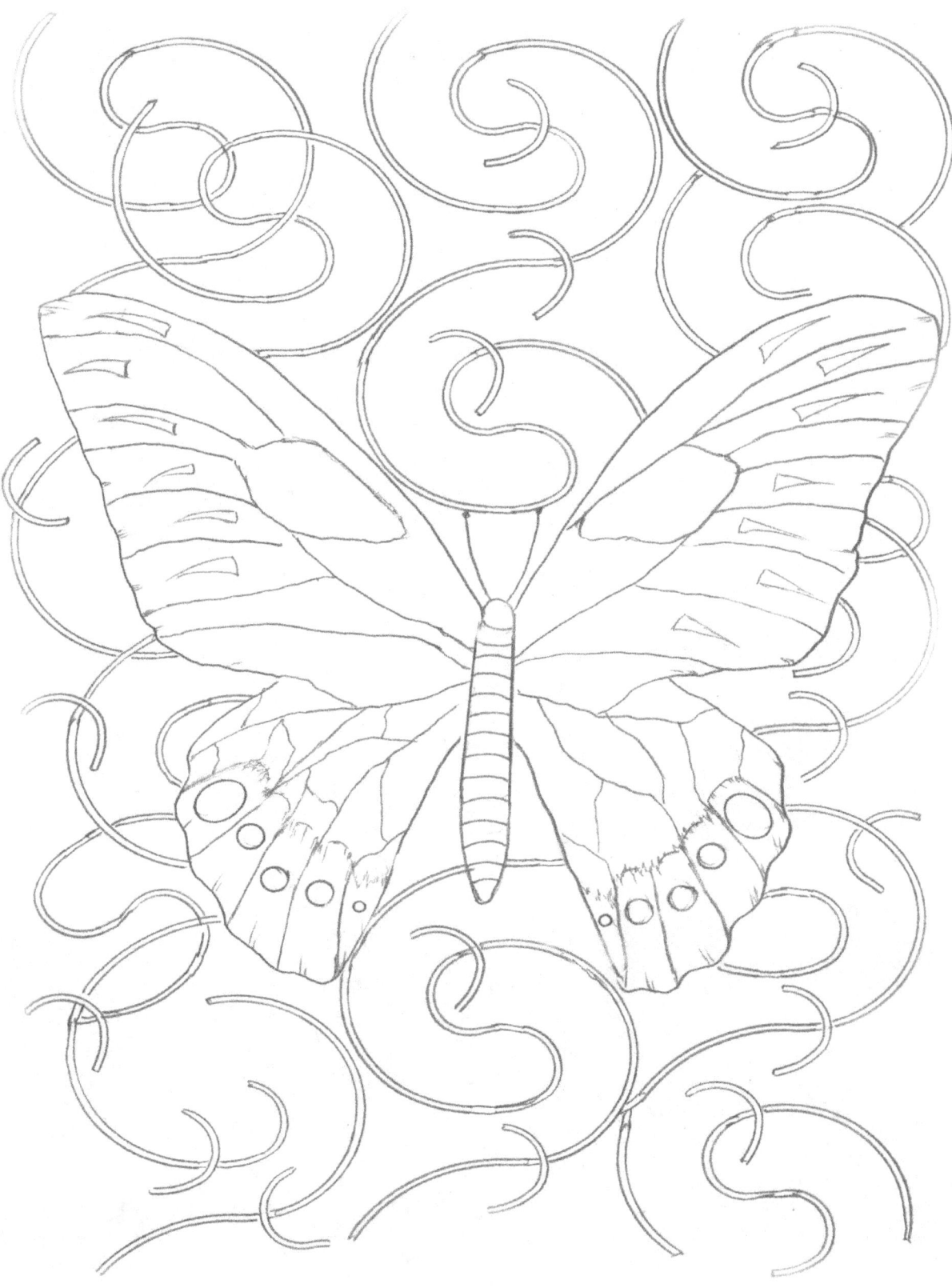

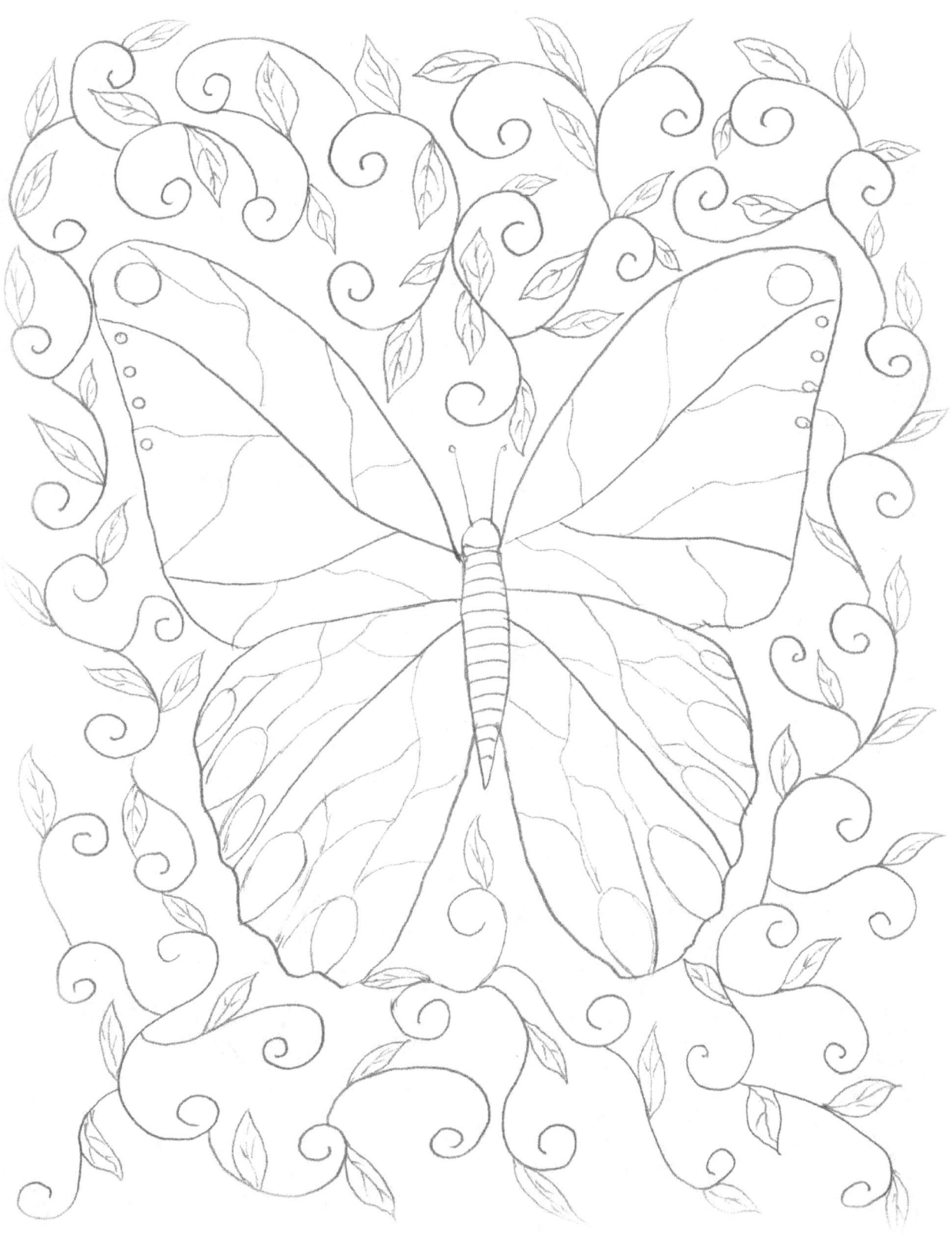

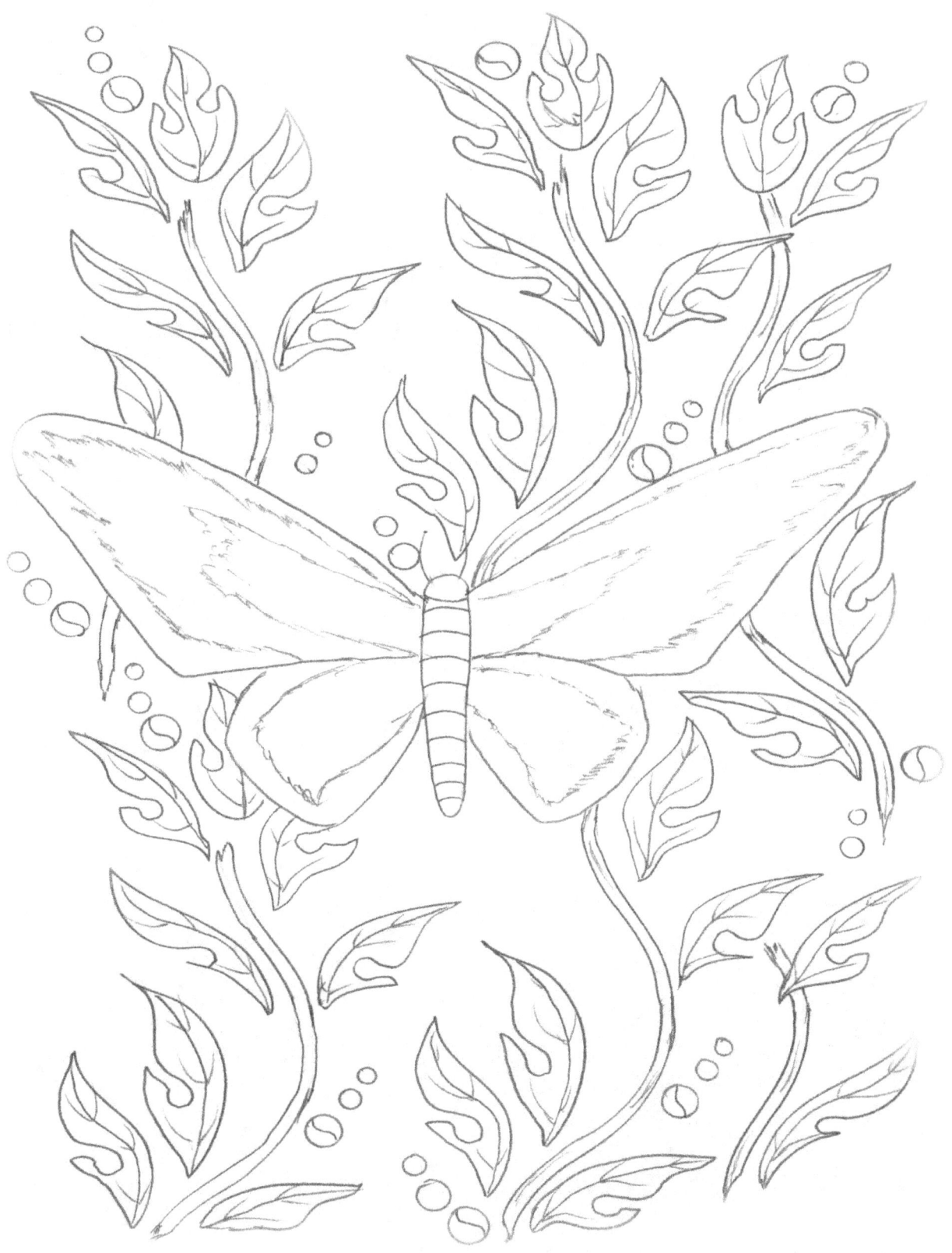

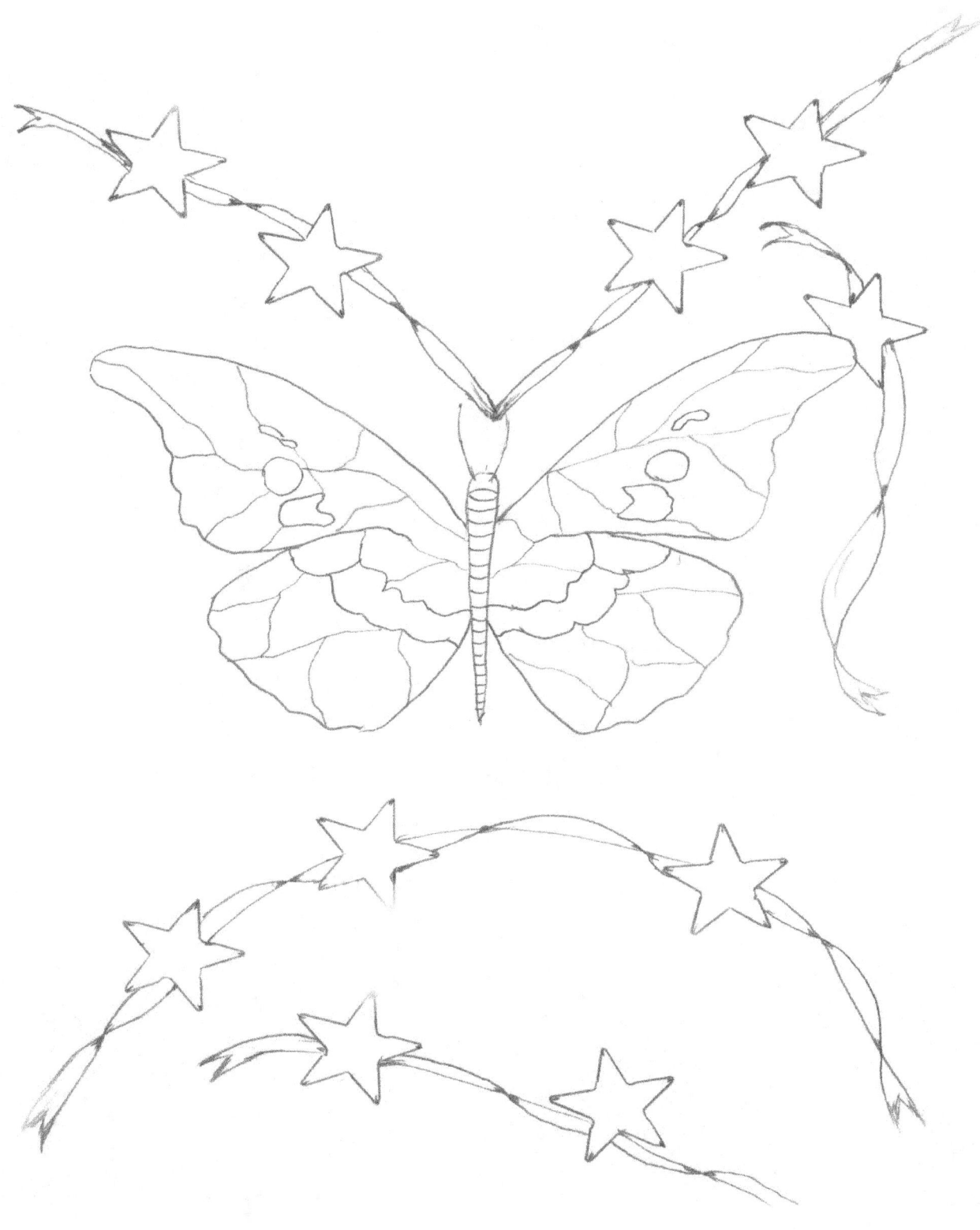

Carol Hopkins

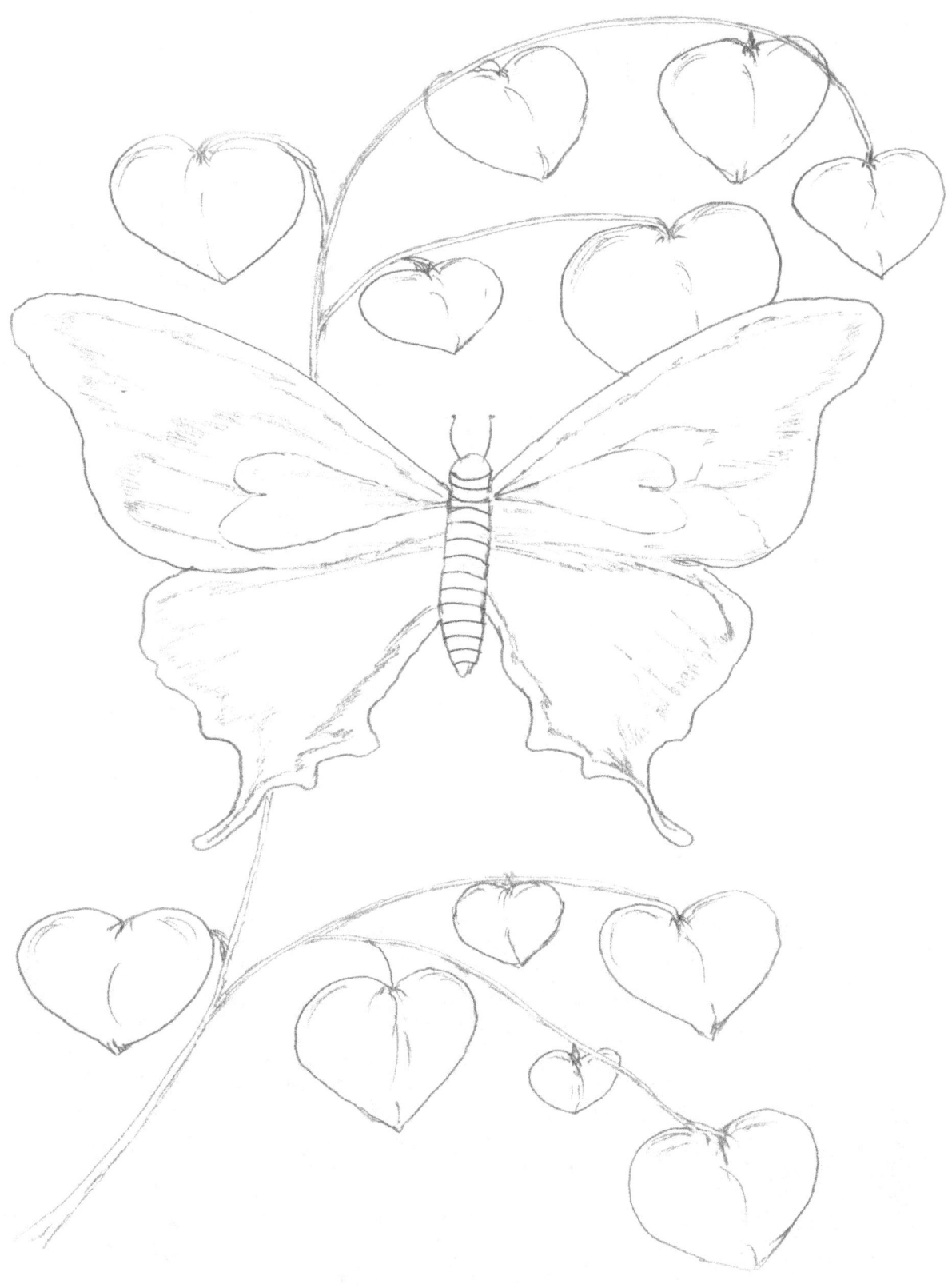

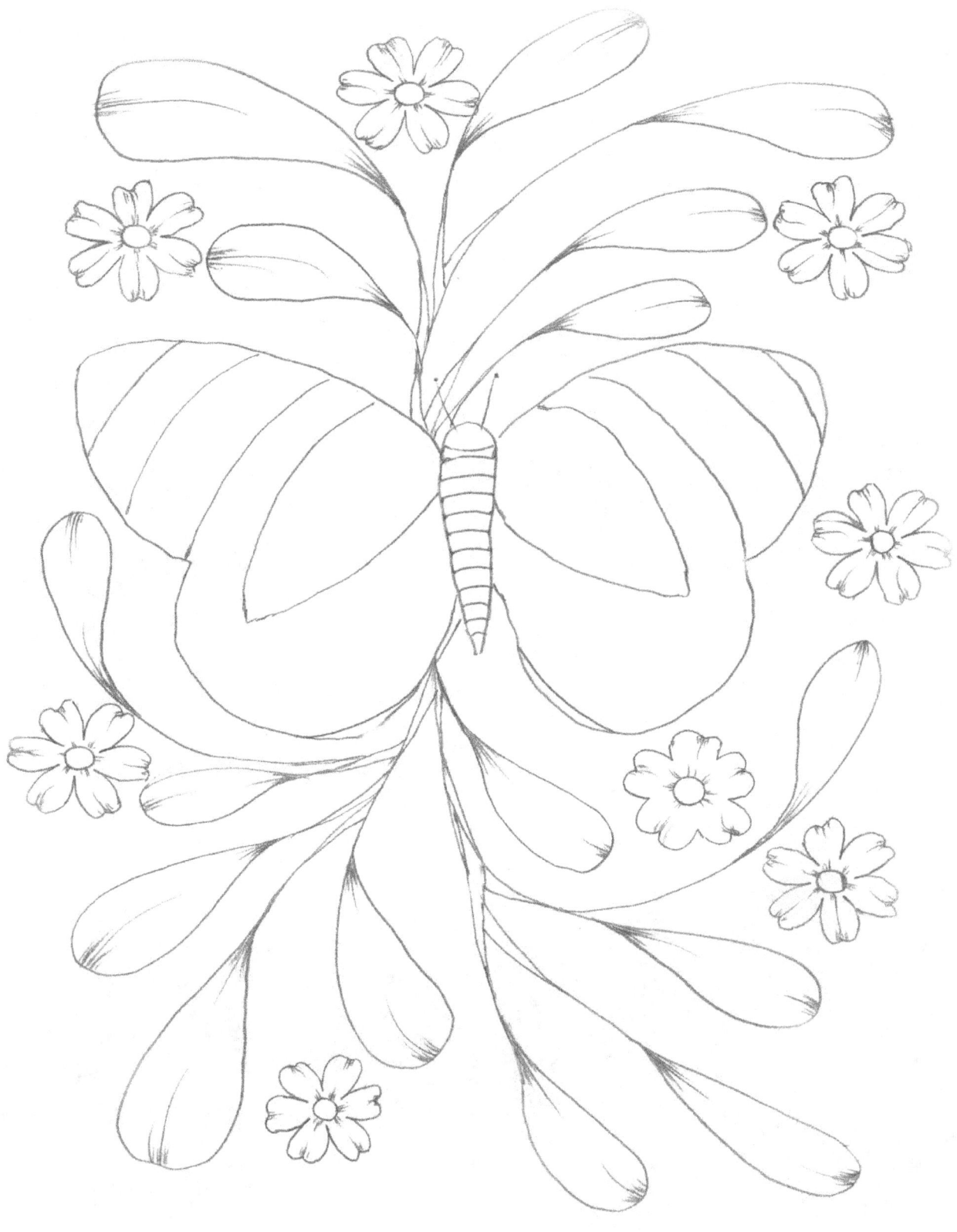

Carol Hopkins

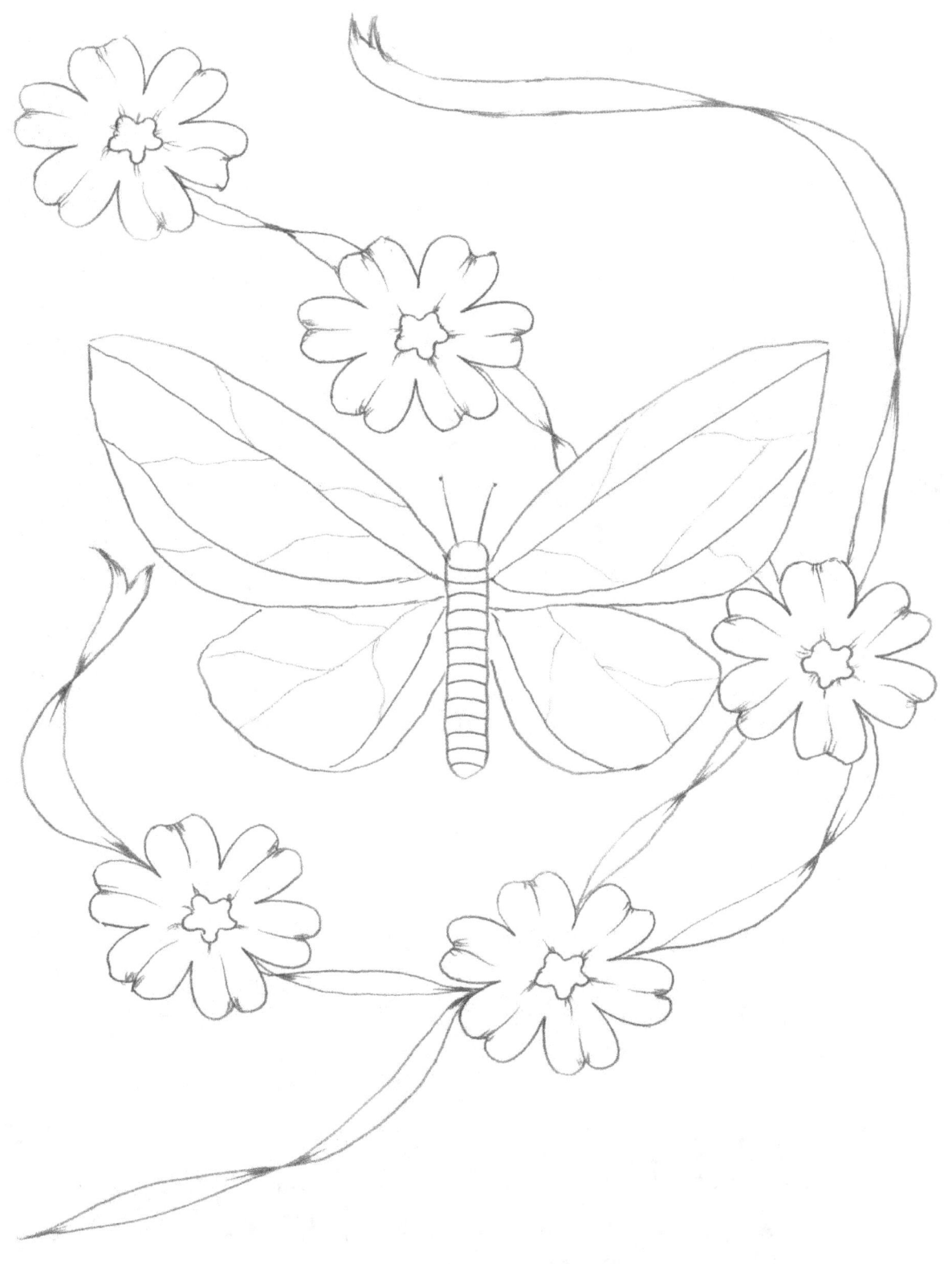

Relaxation

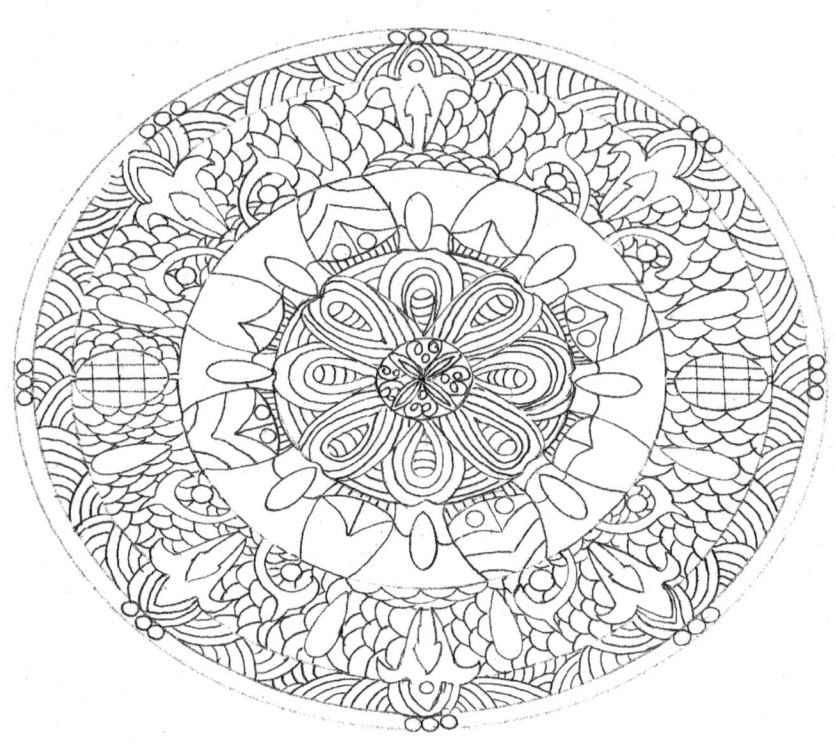

Carol Hopkins

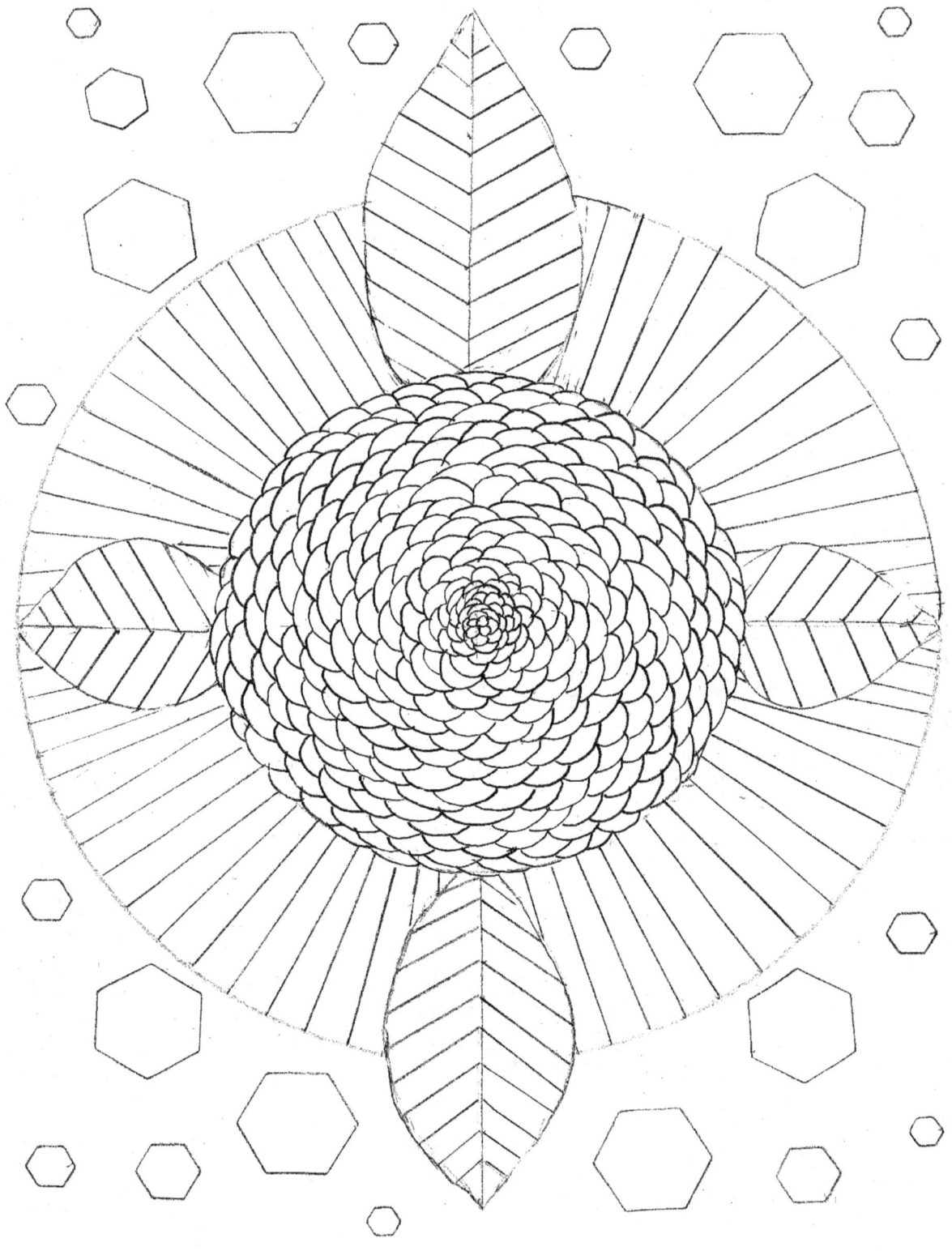

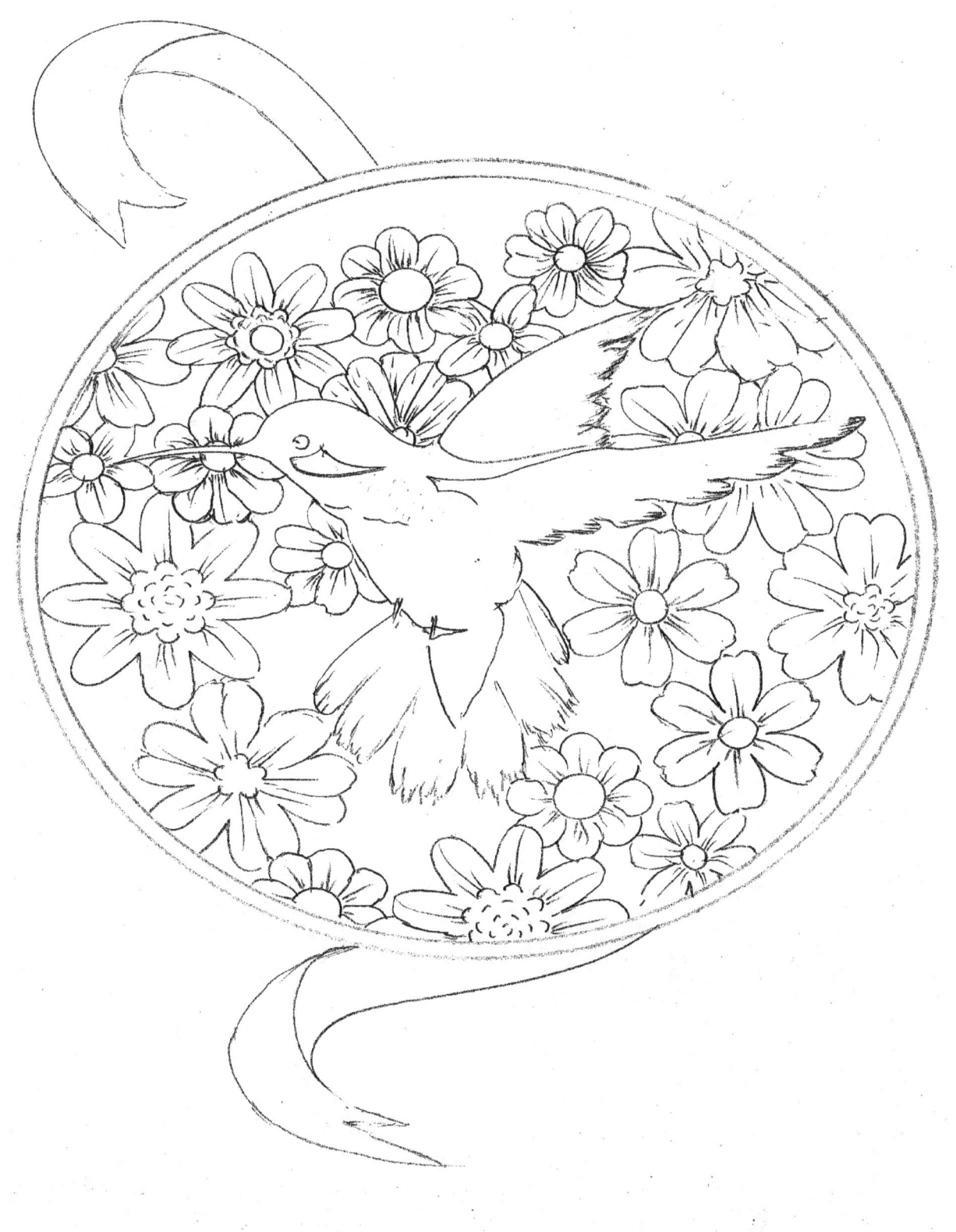

Carol Hopkins

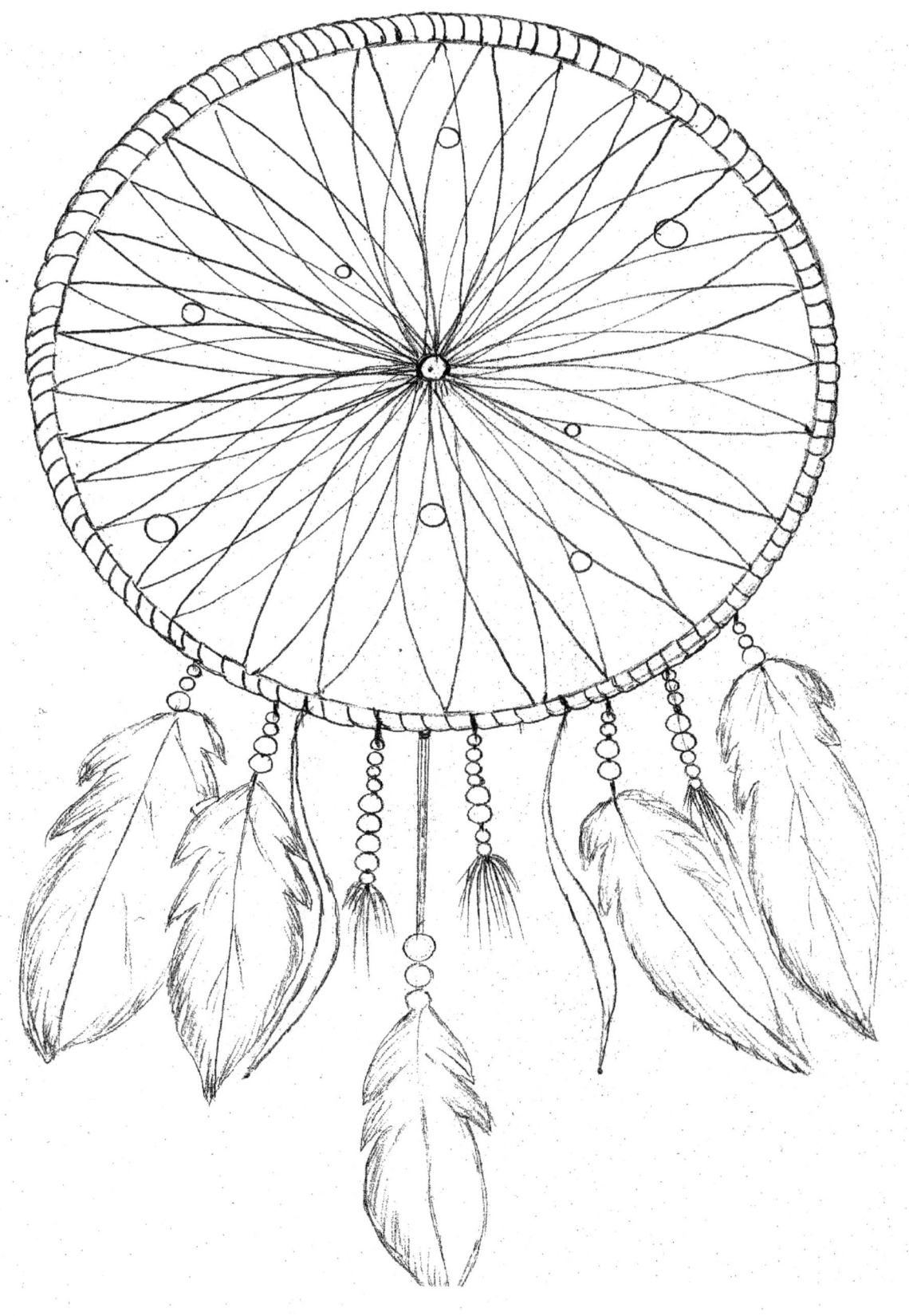

Carol Hopkins

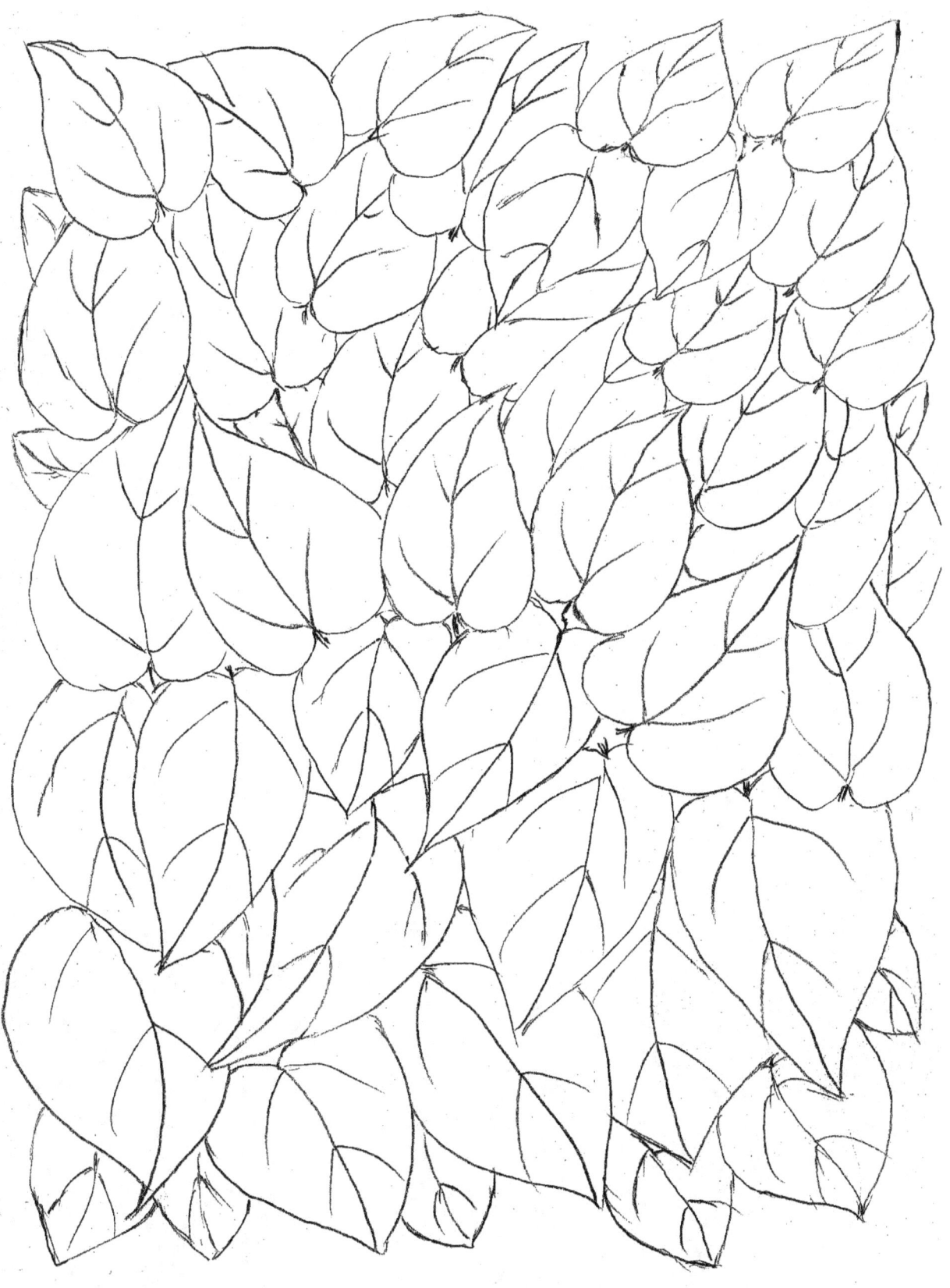

Carol Hopkins

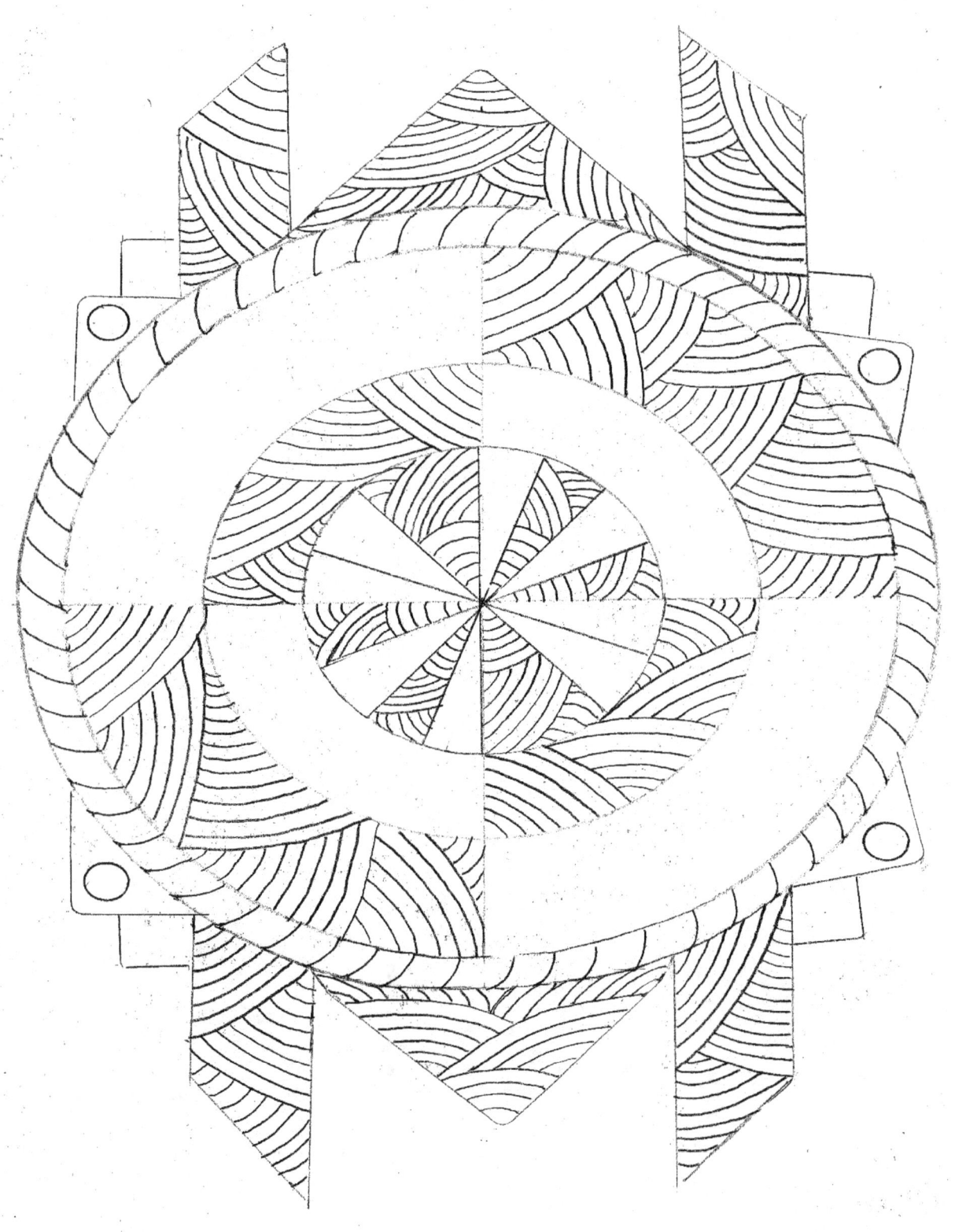

Carol Hopkins

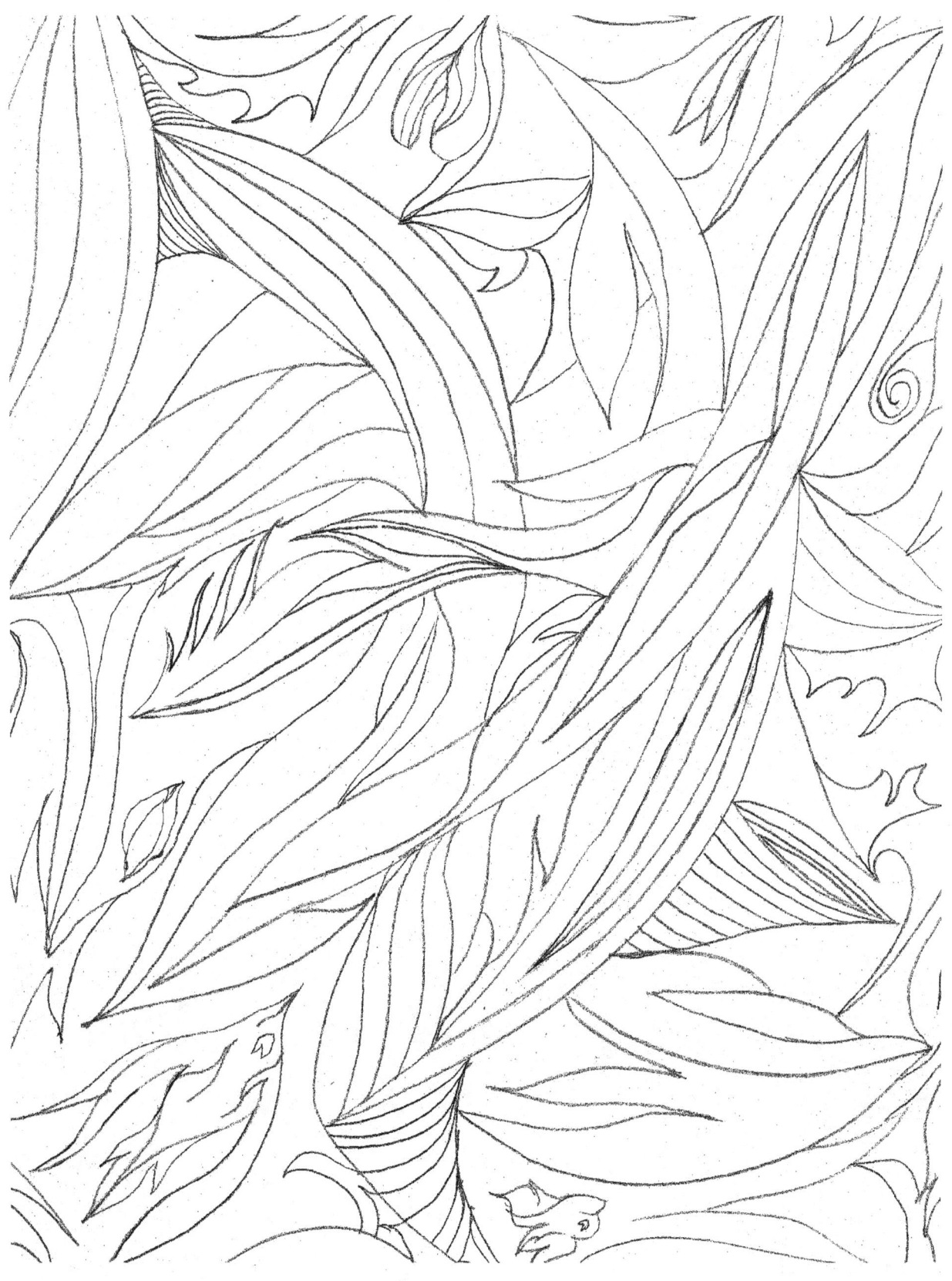

Carol Hopkins

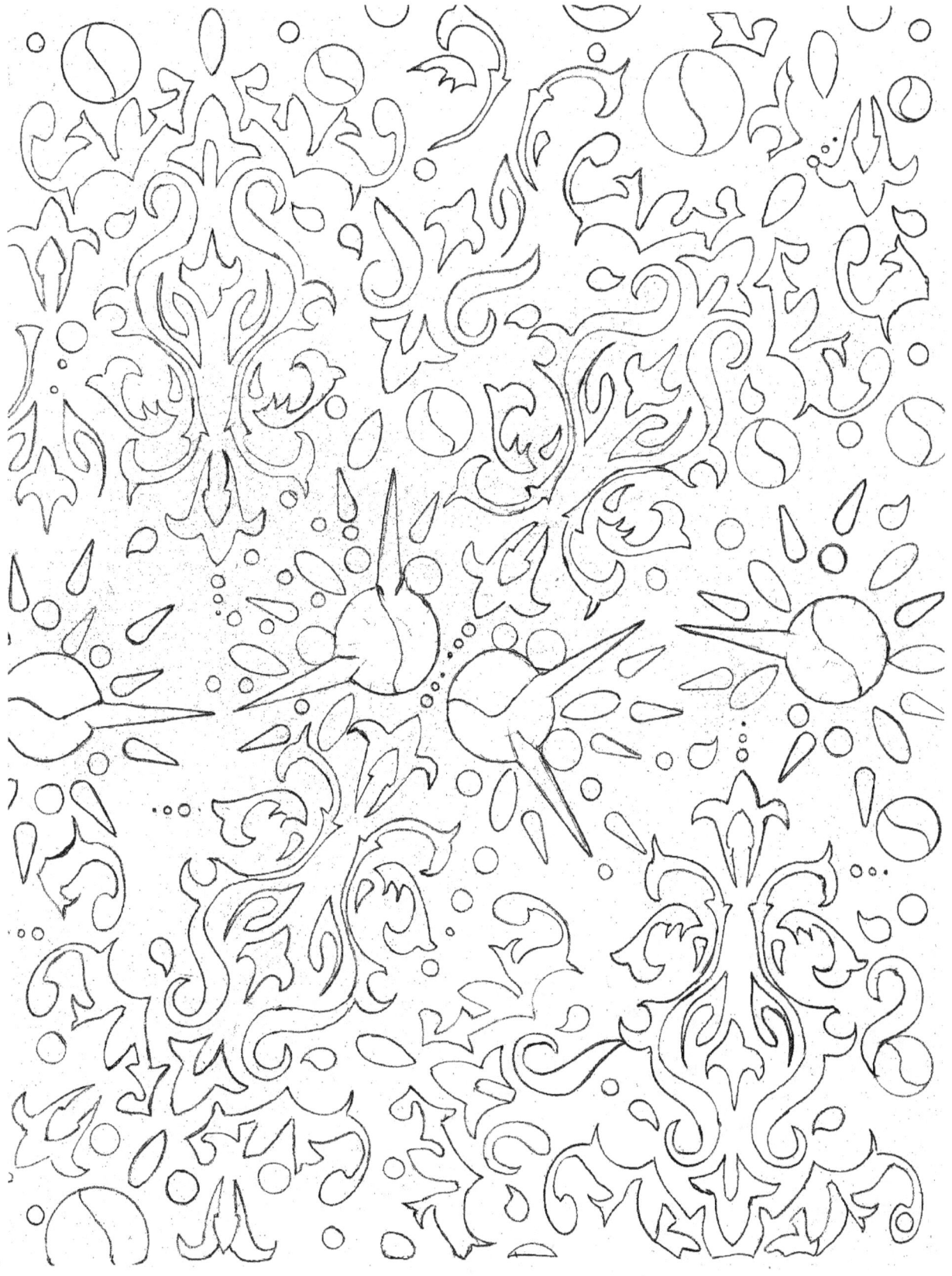

Carol Hopkins

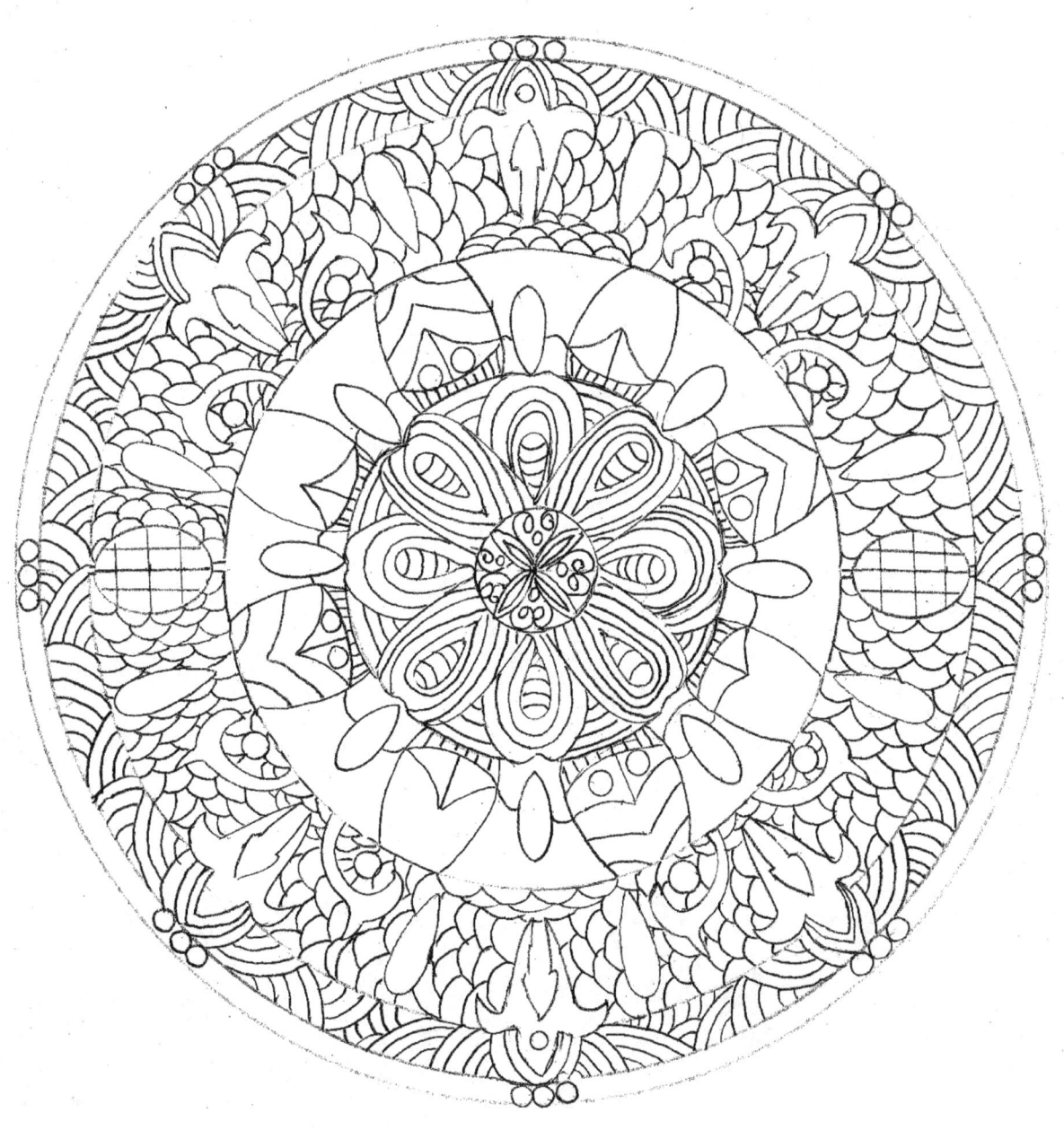

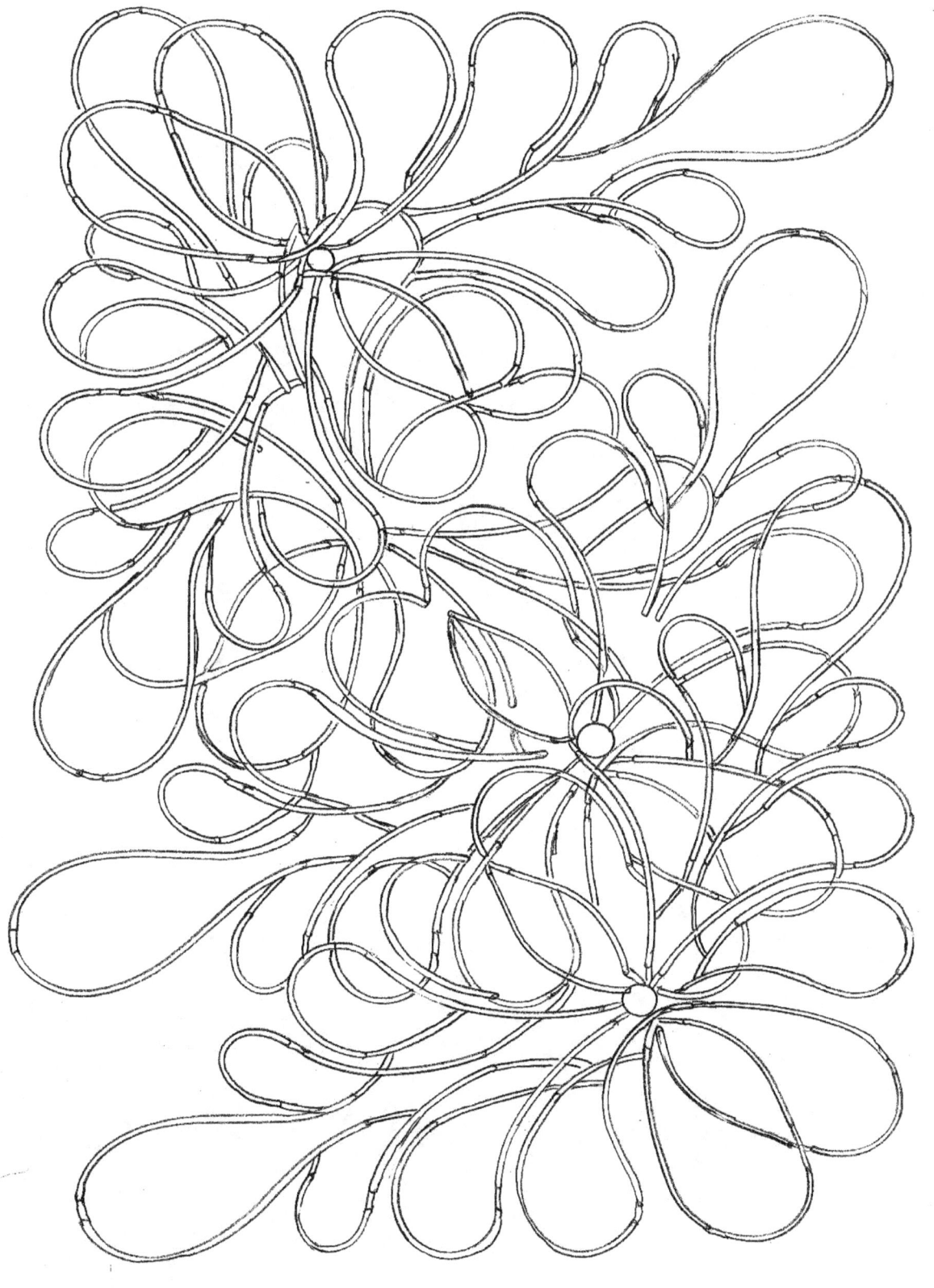

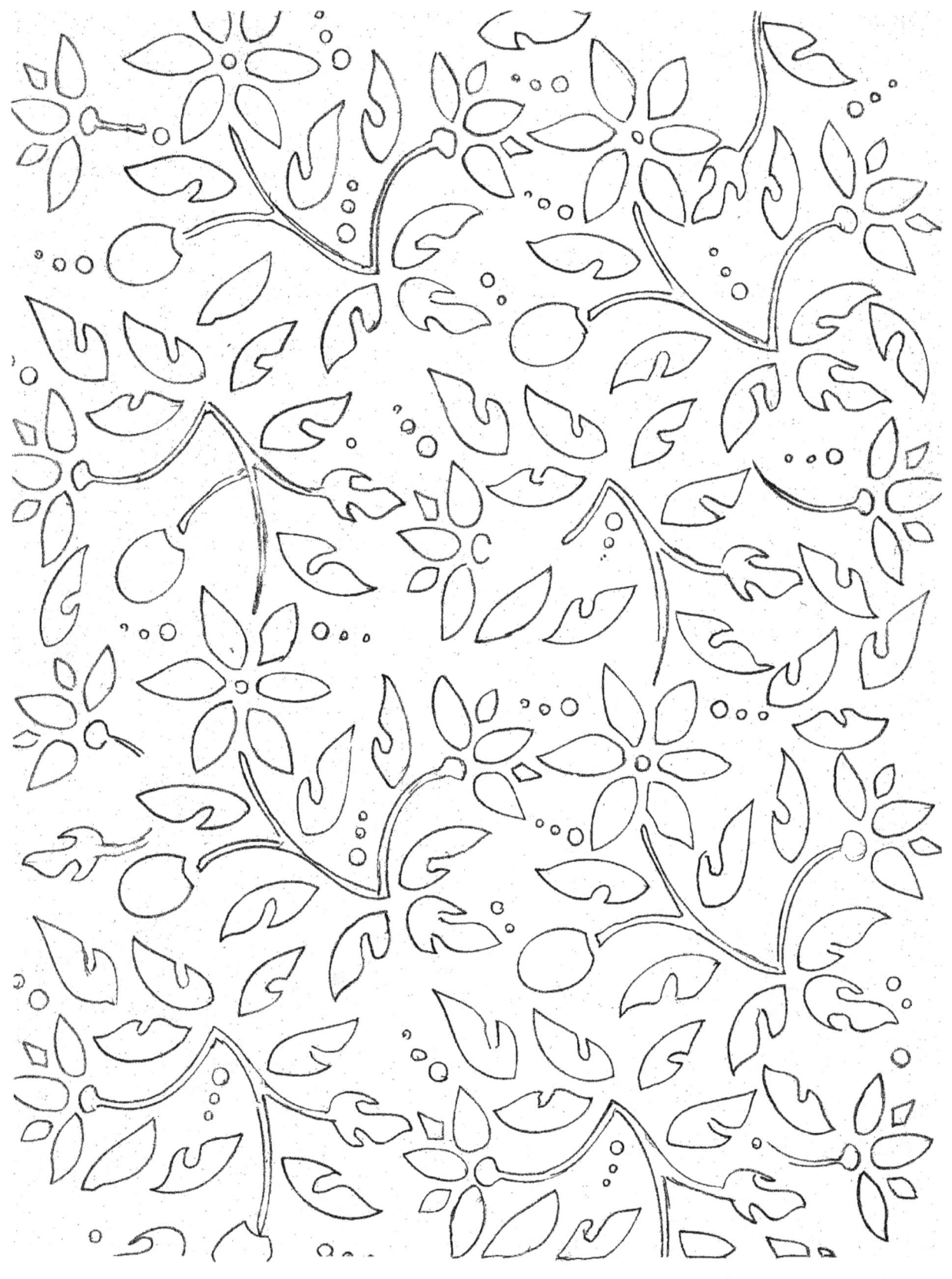

Carol Hopkins

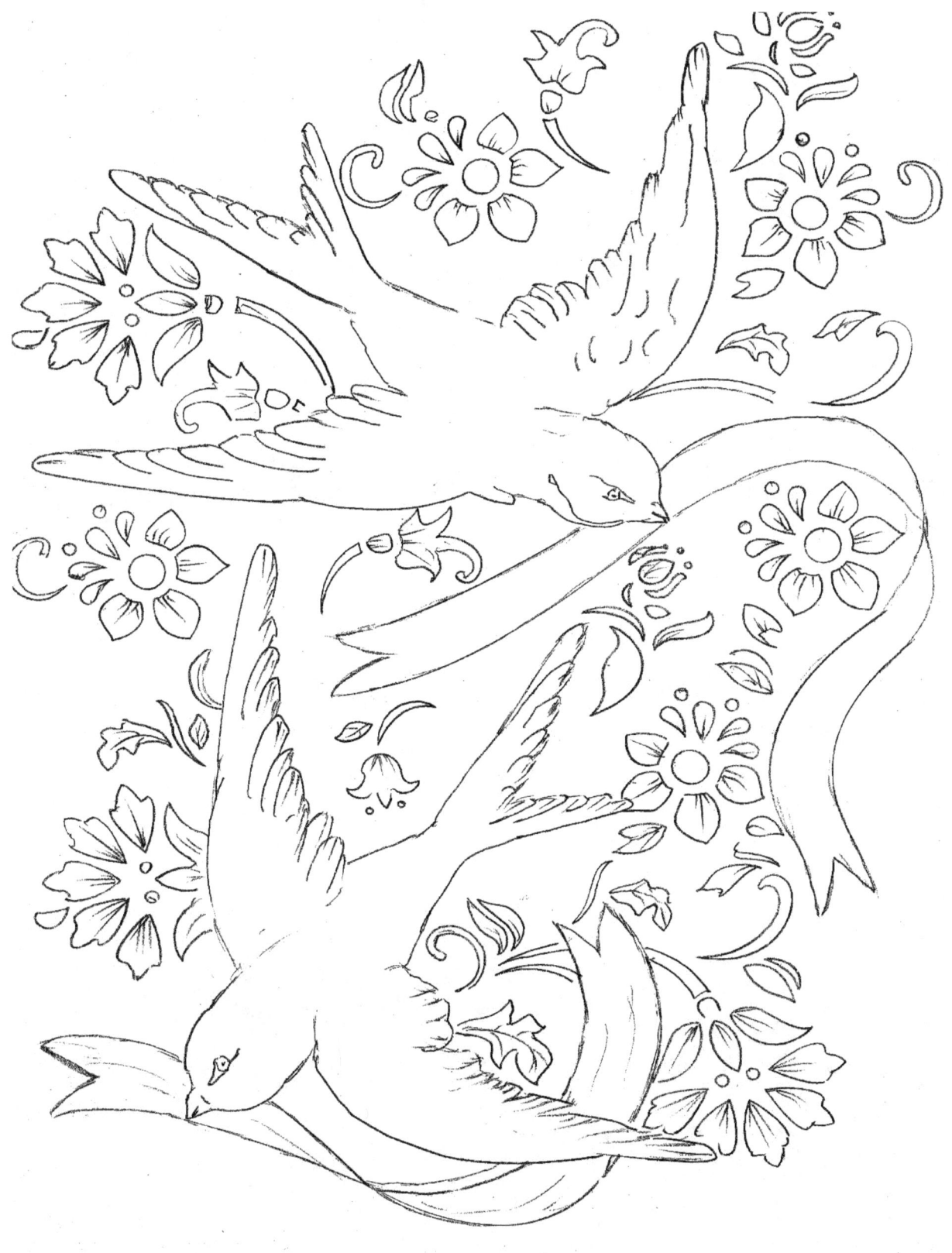

Carol Hopkins

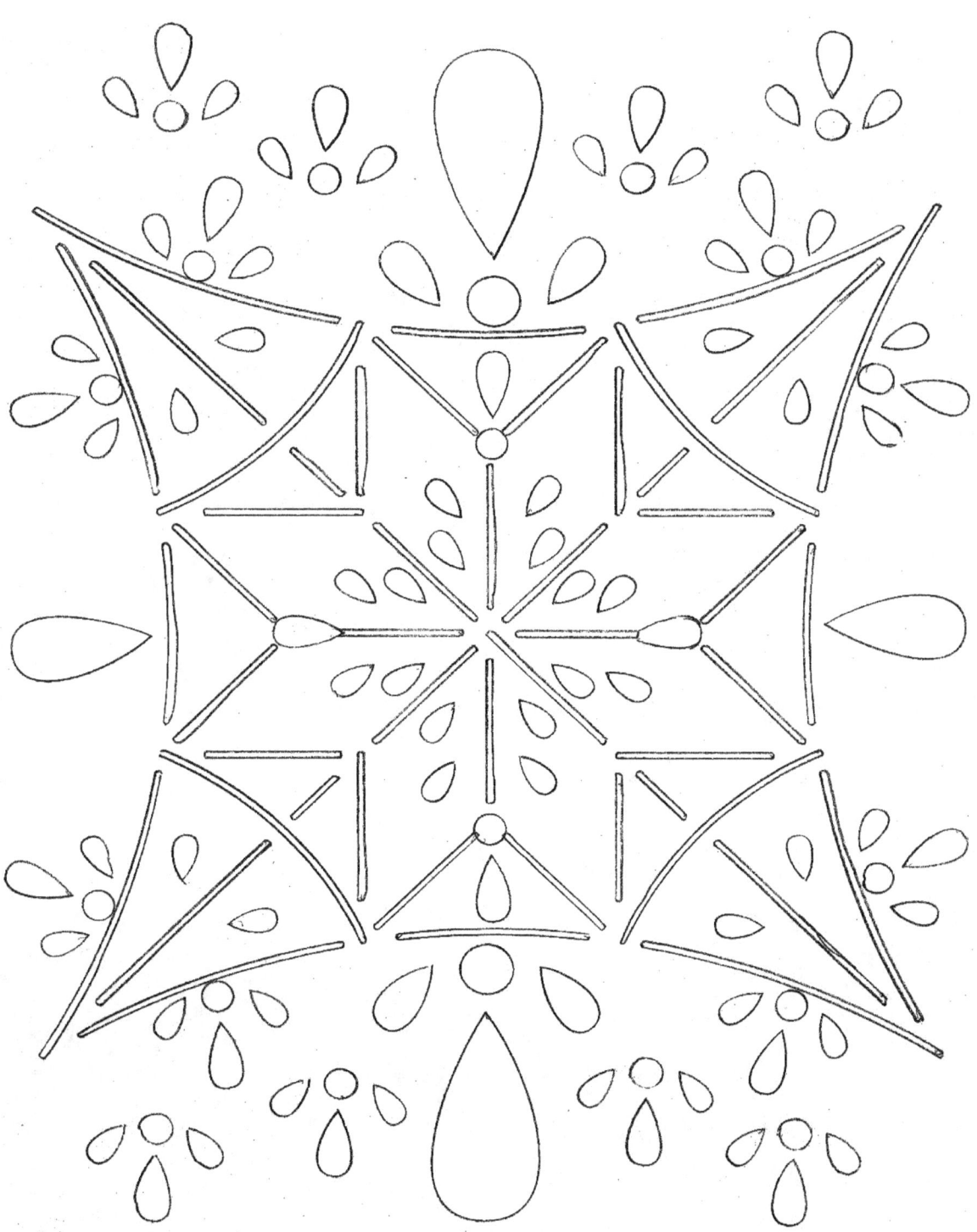

Carol Hopkins

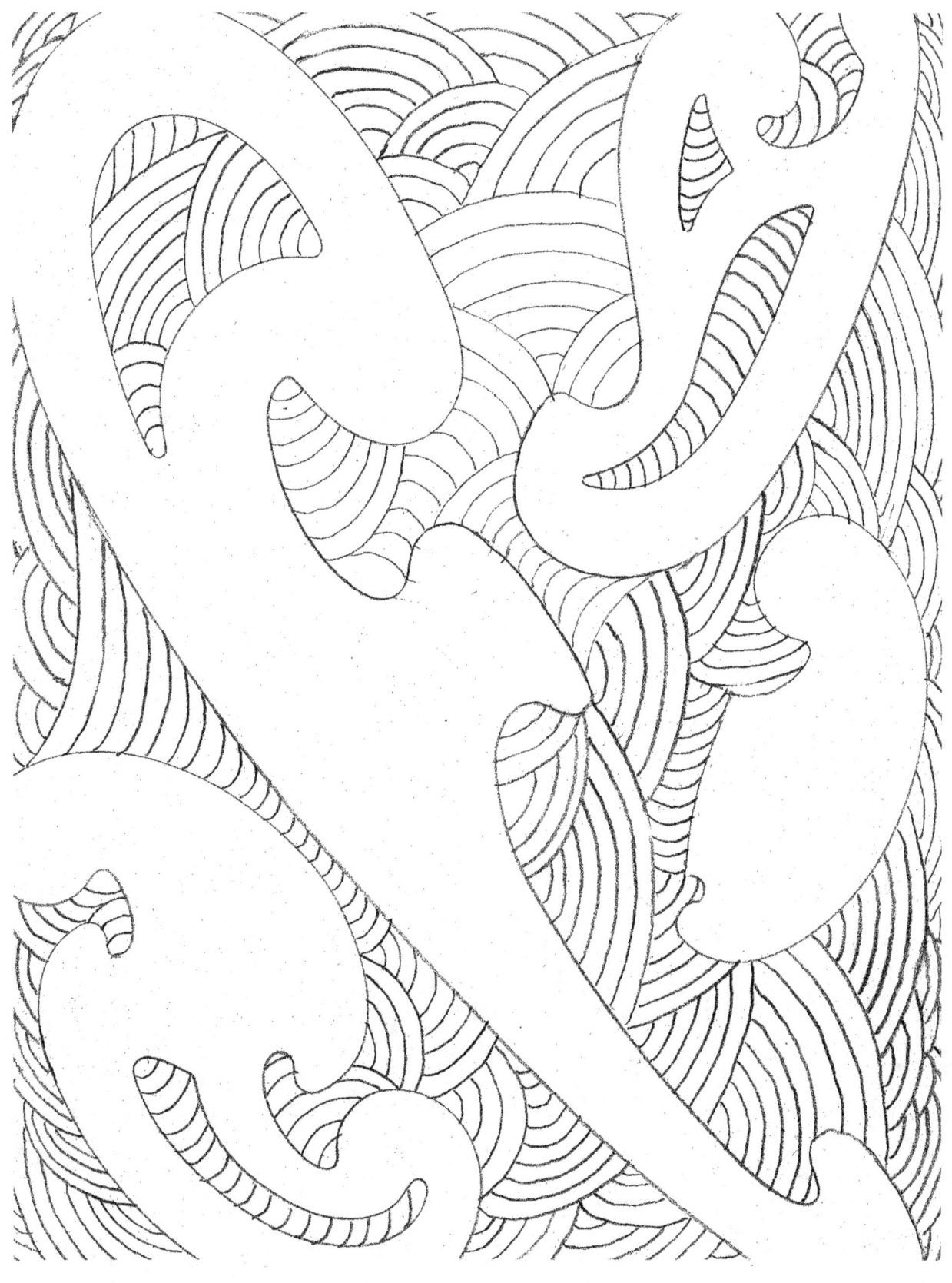

Carol Hopkins

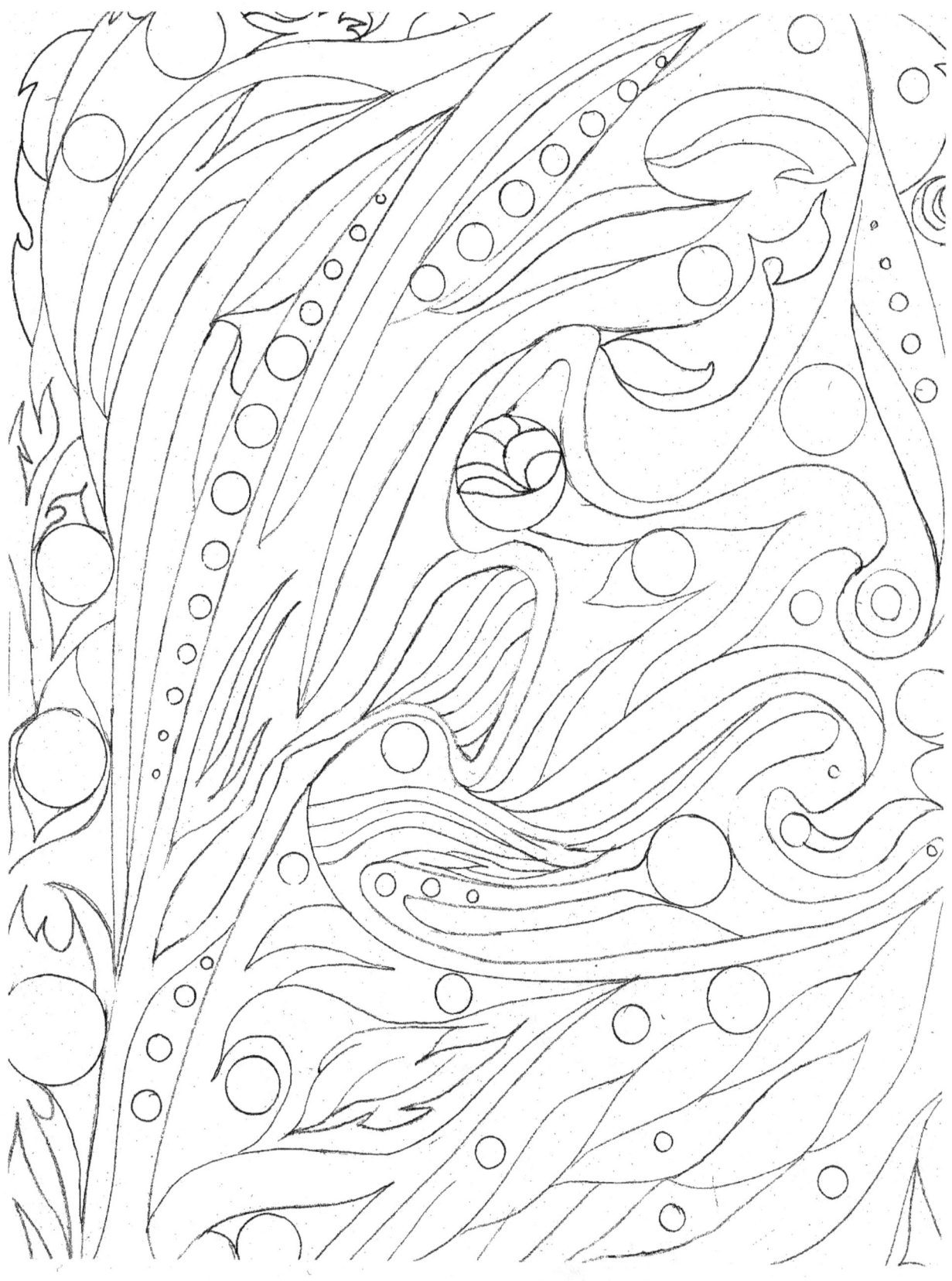

Carol Hopkins

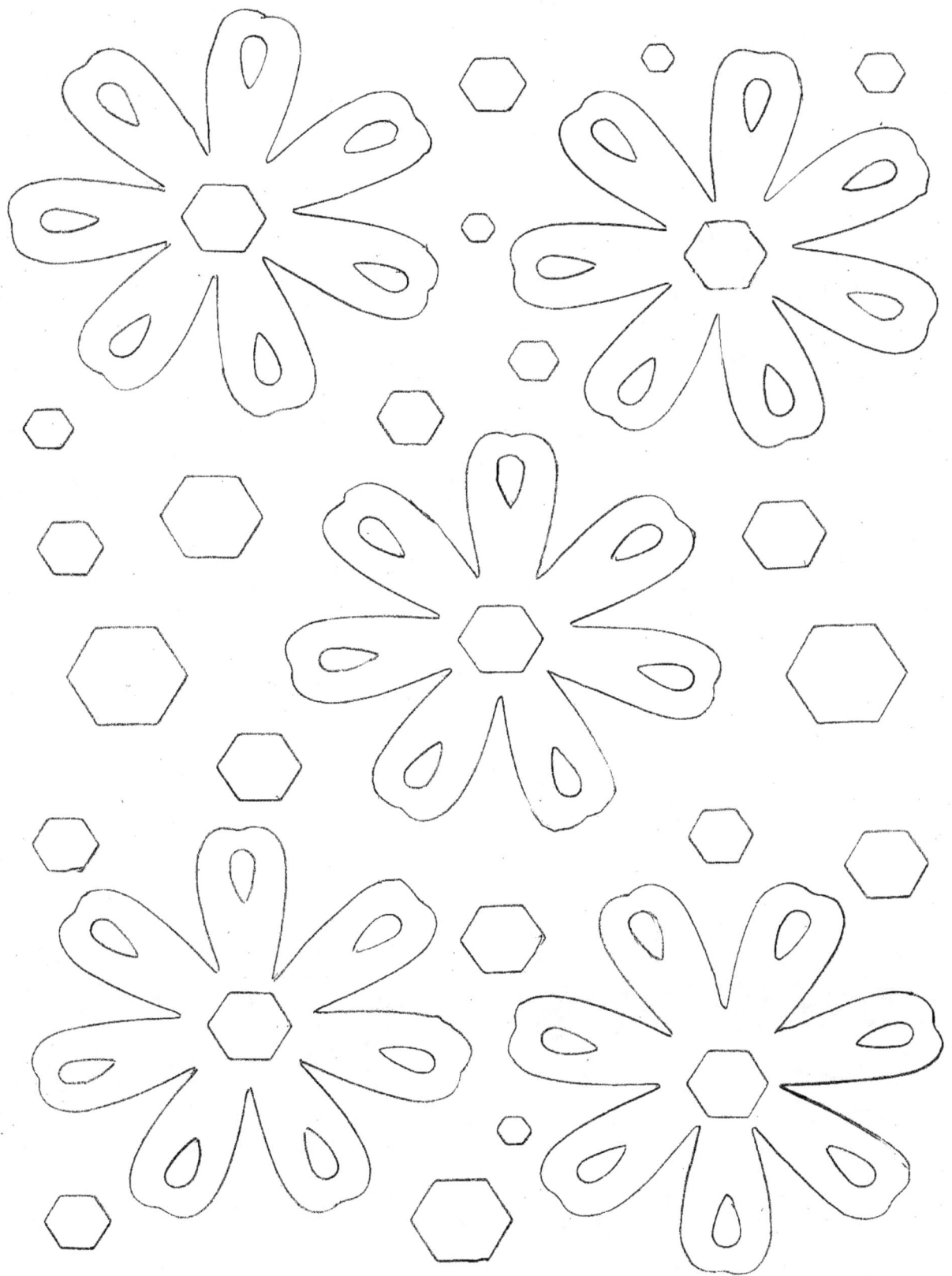

Carol Hopkins

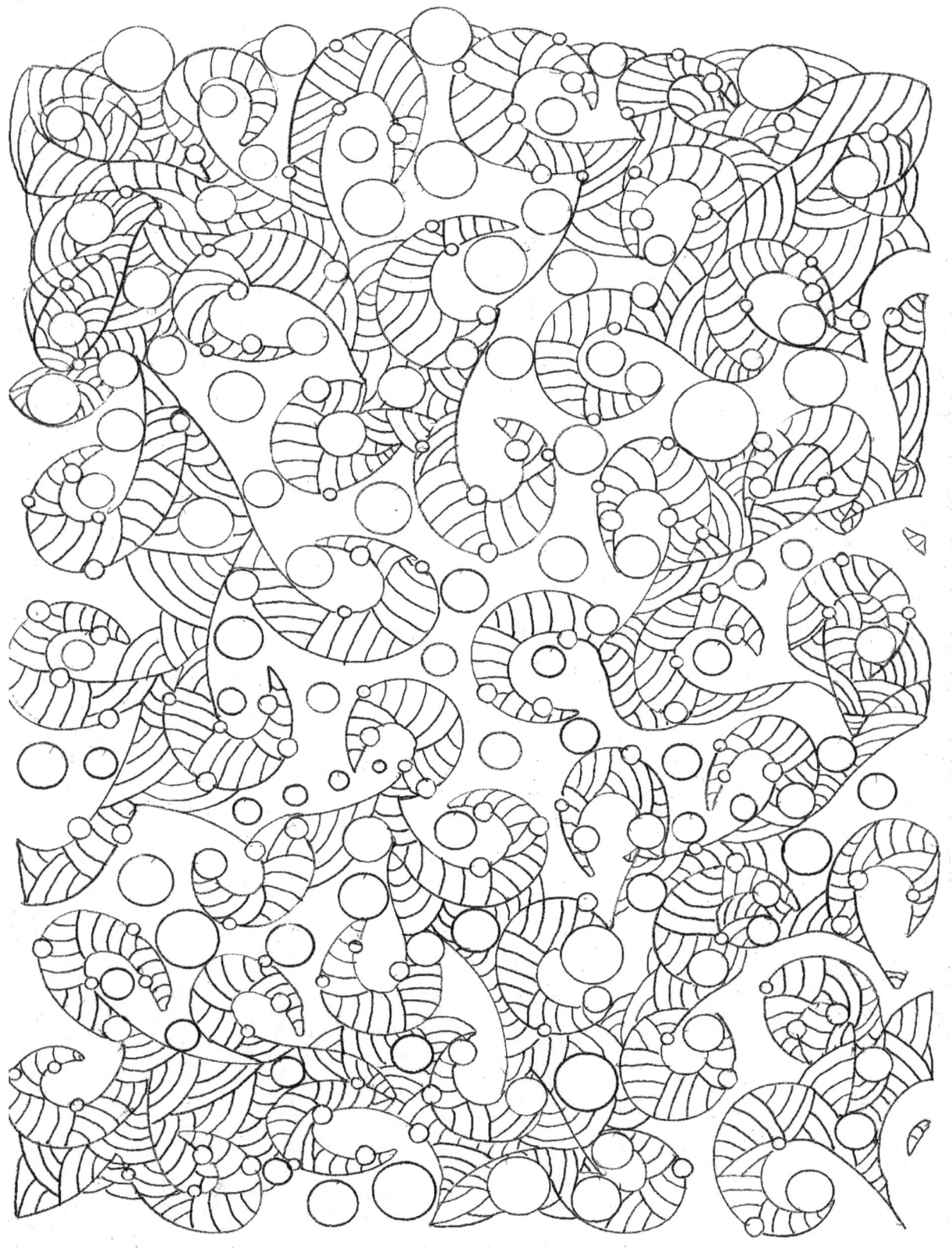

Carol Hopkins

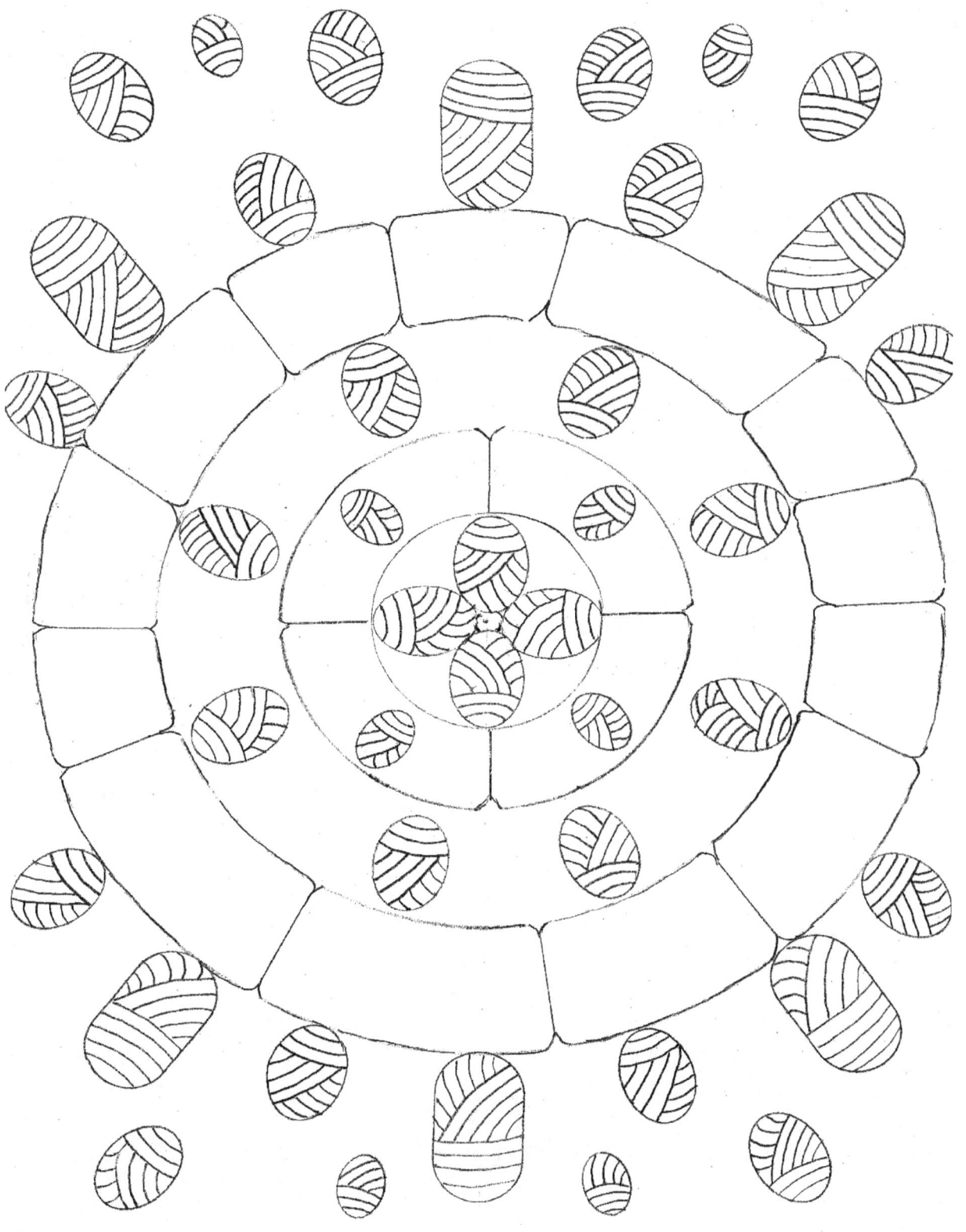

Carol Hopkins

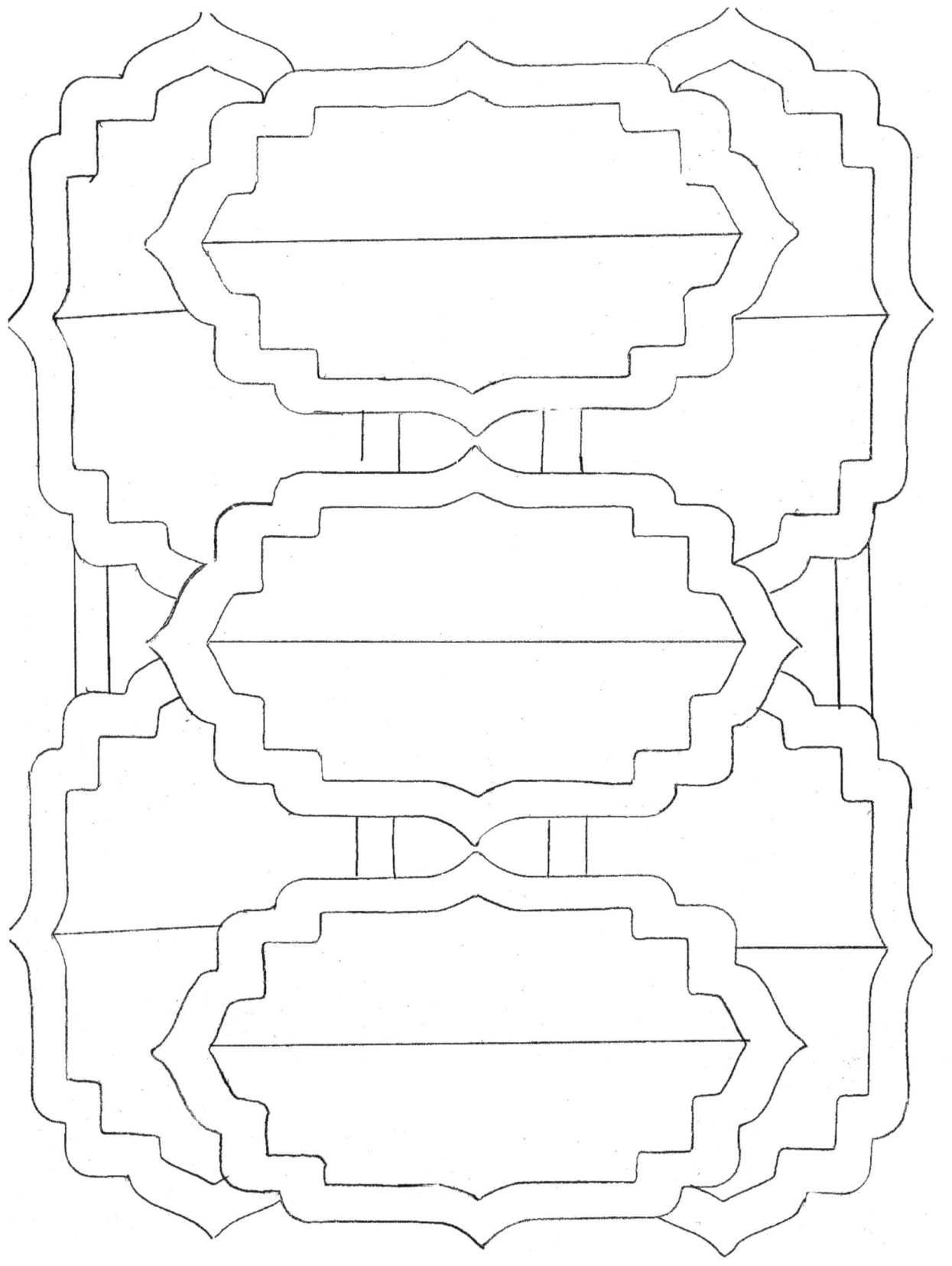

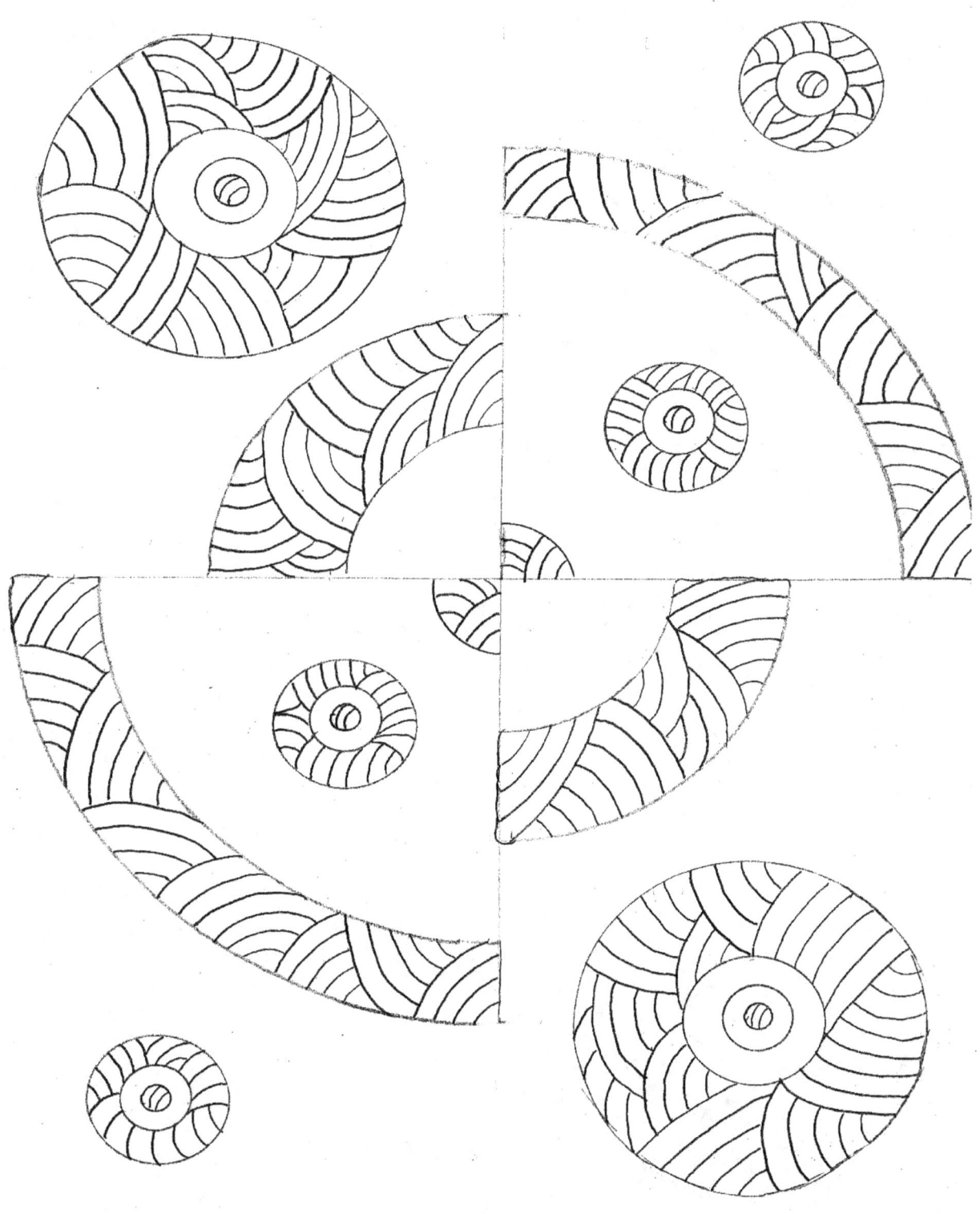

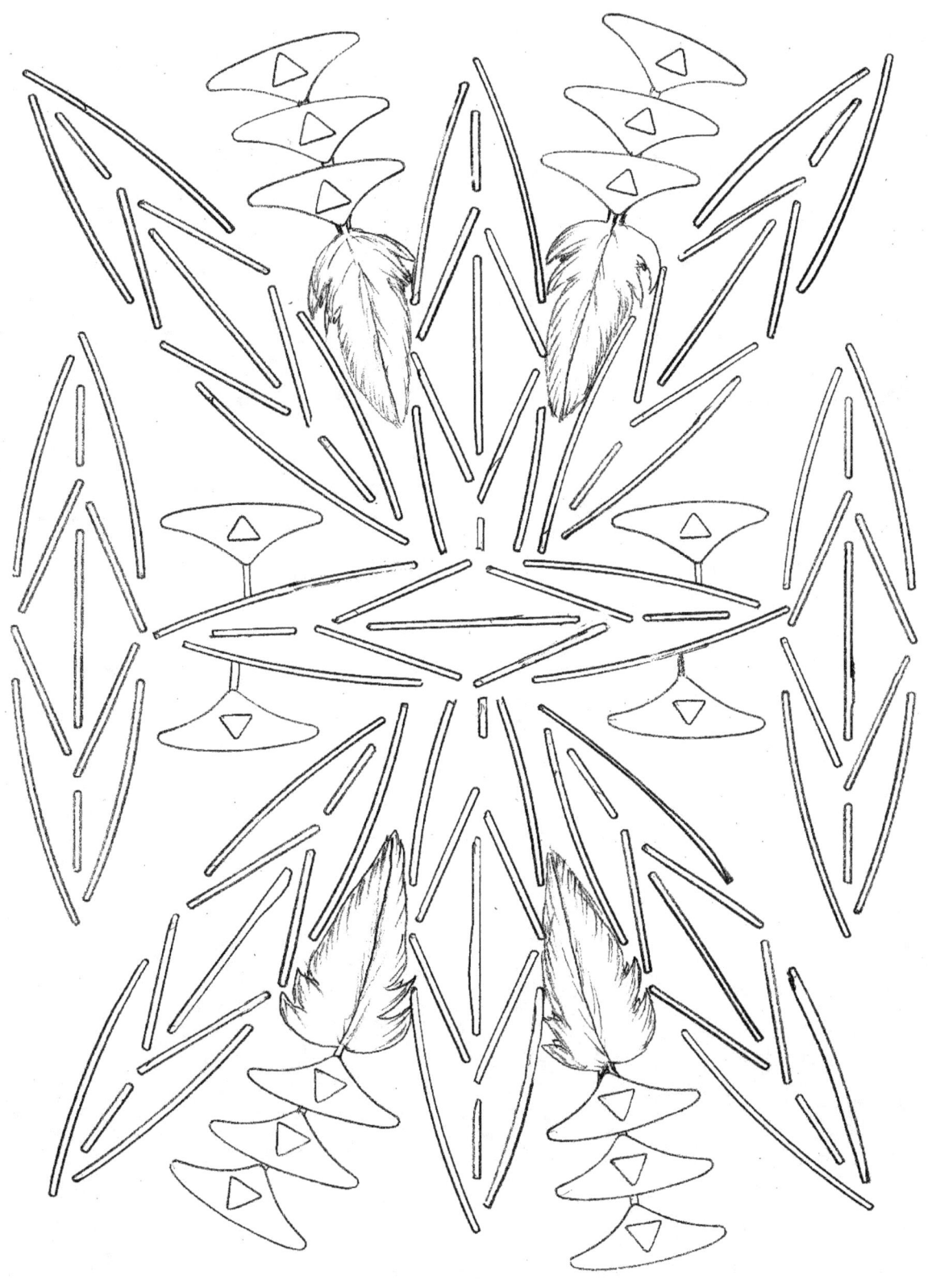

Carol Hopkins

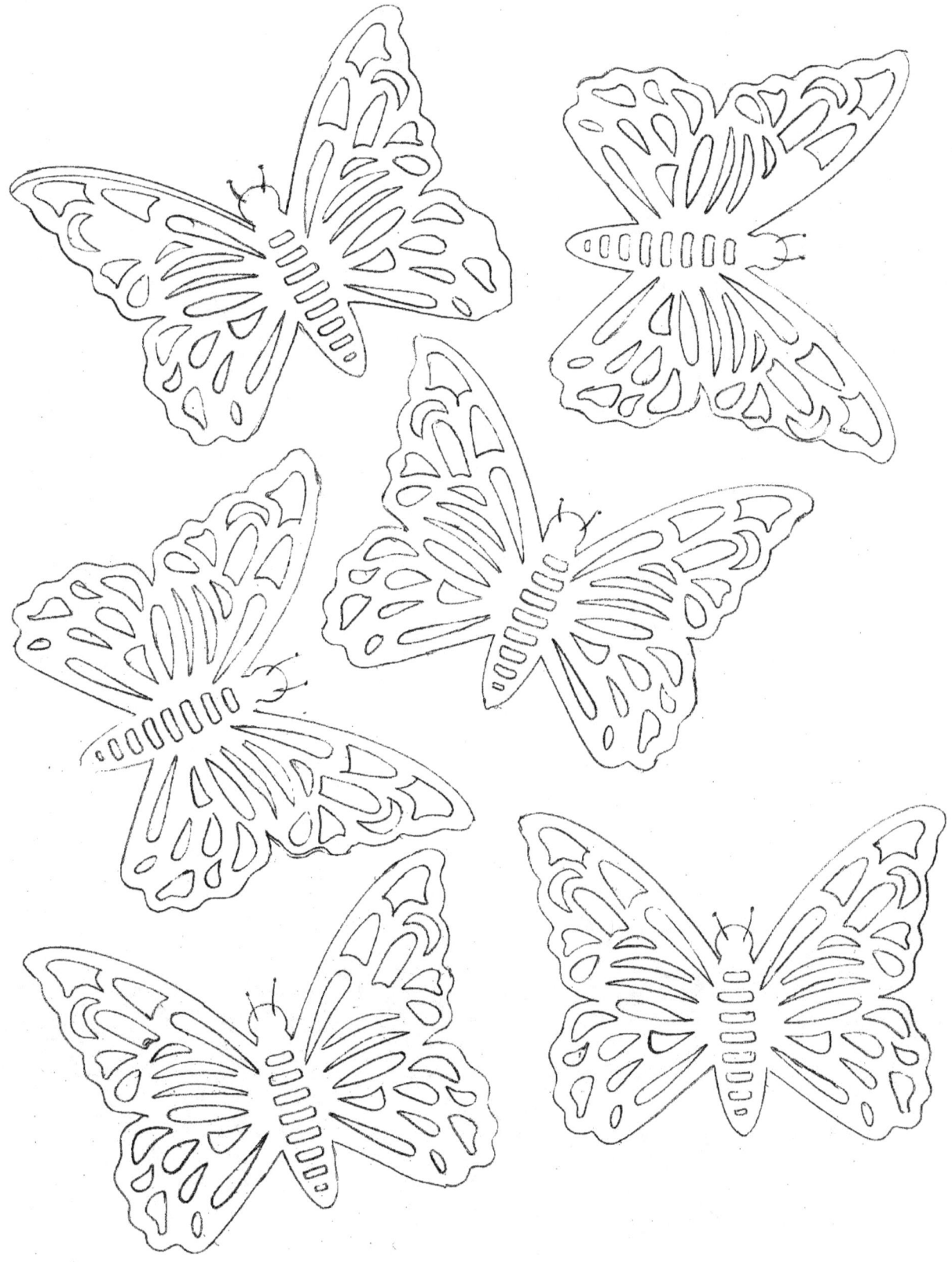

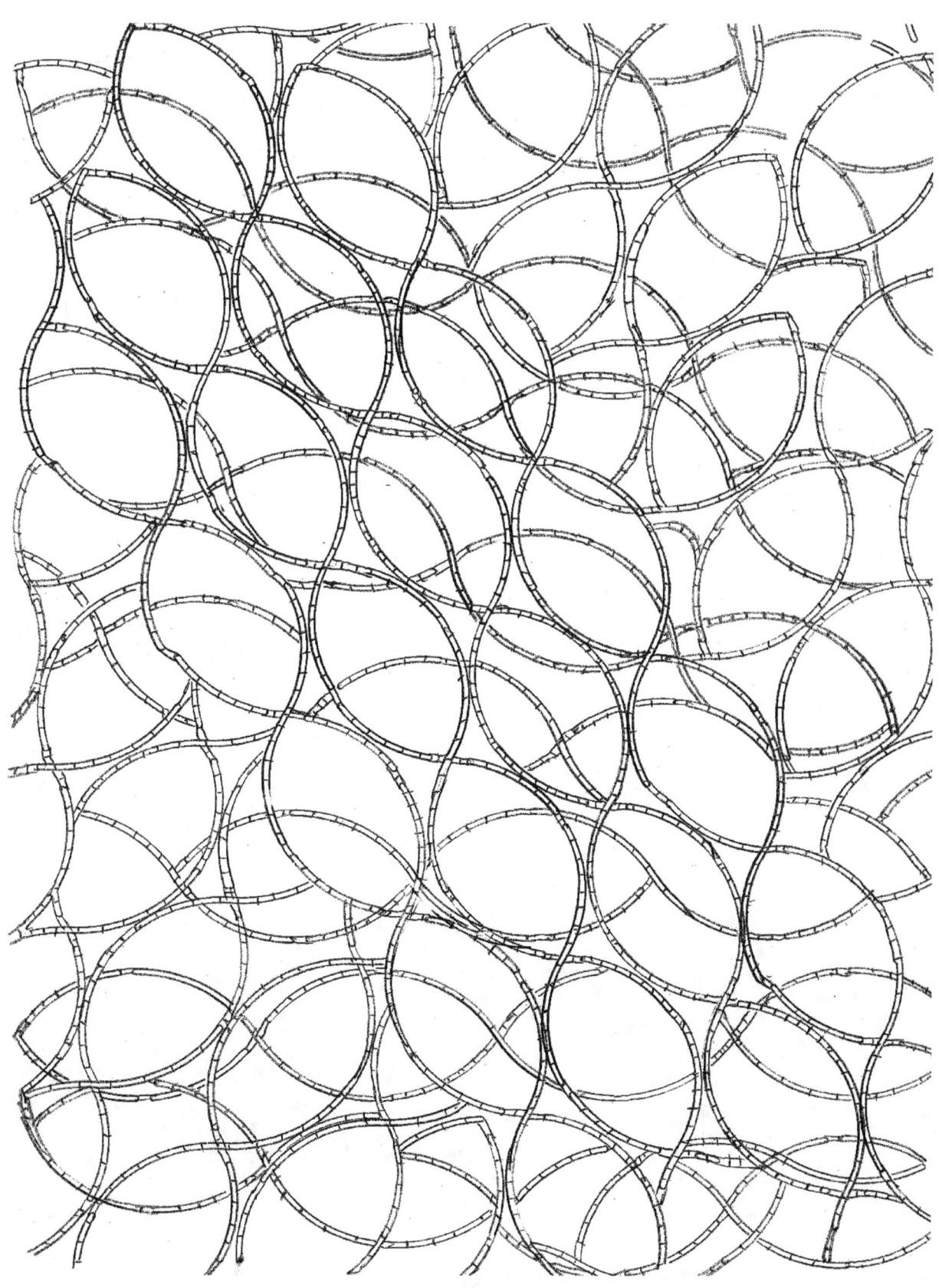

Carol Hopkins

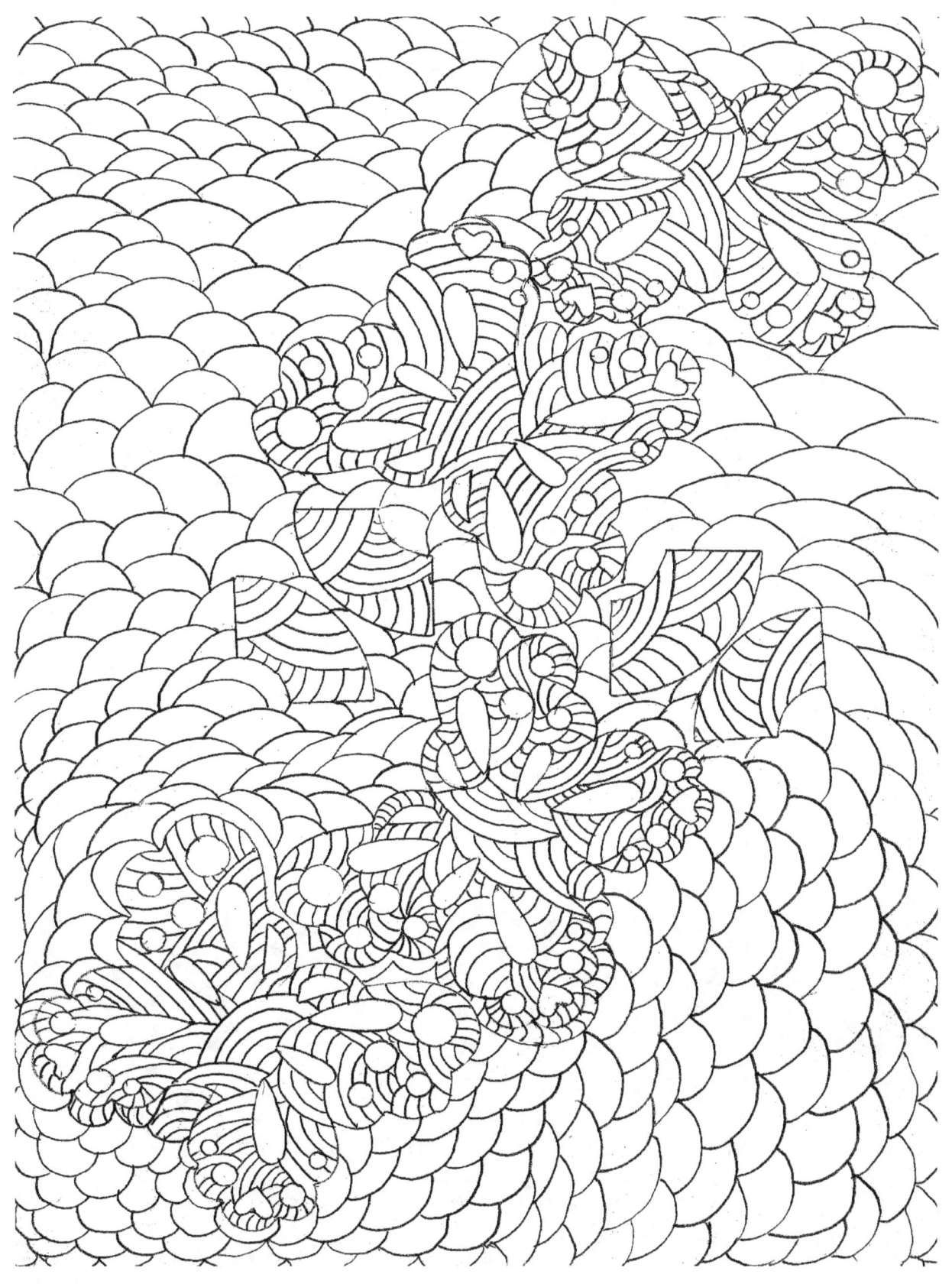

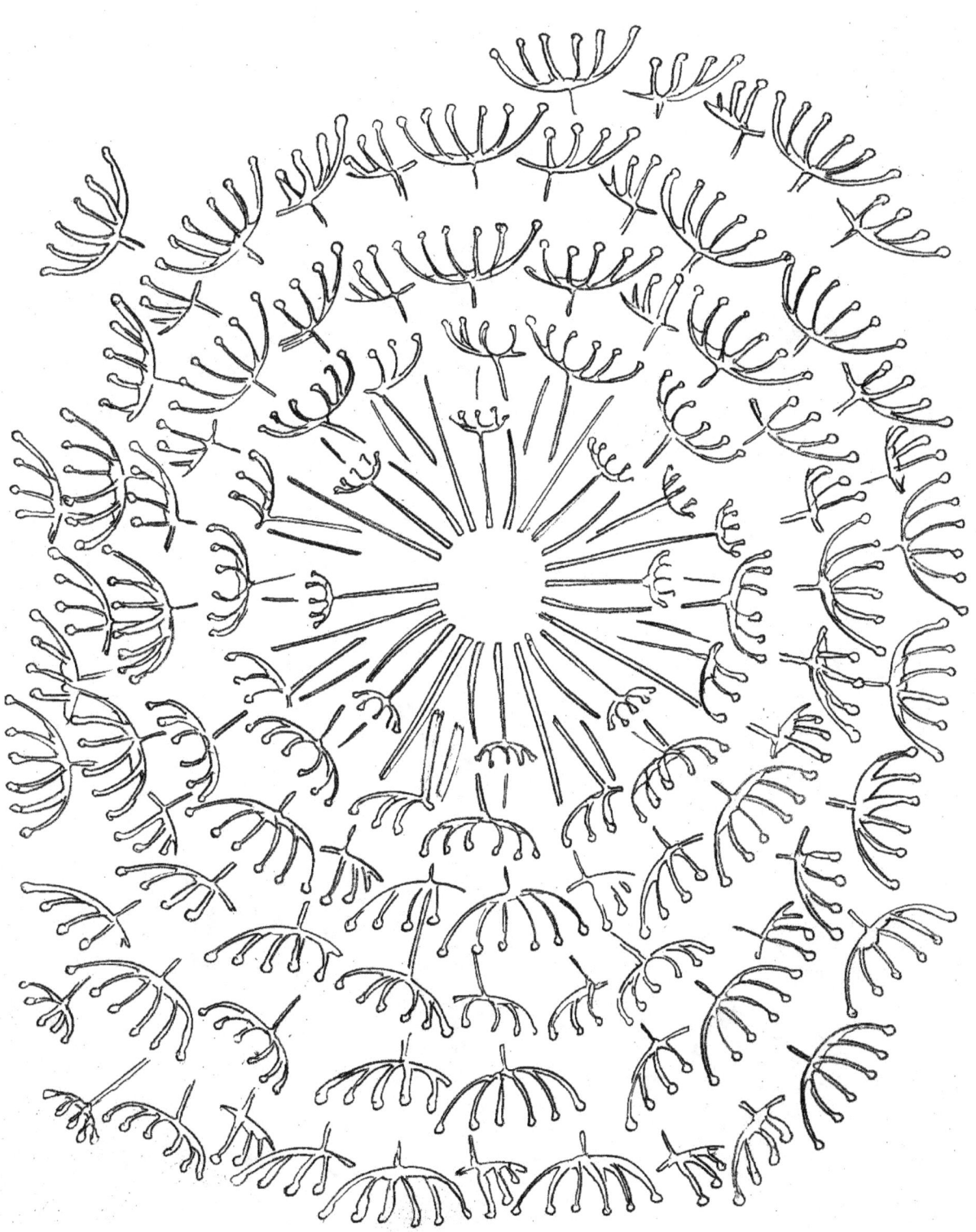

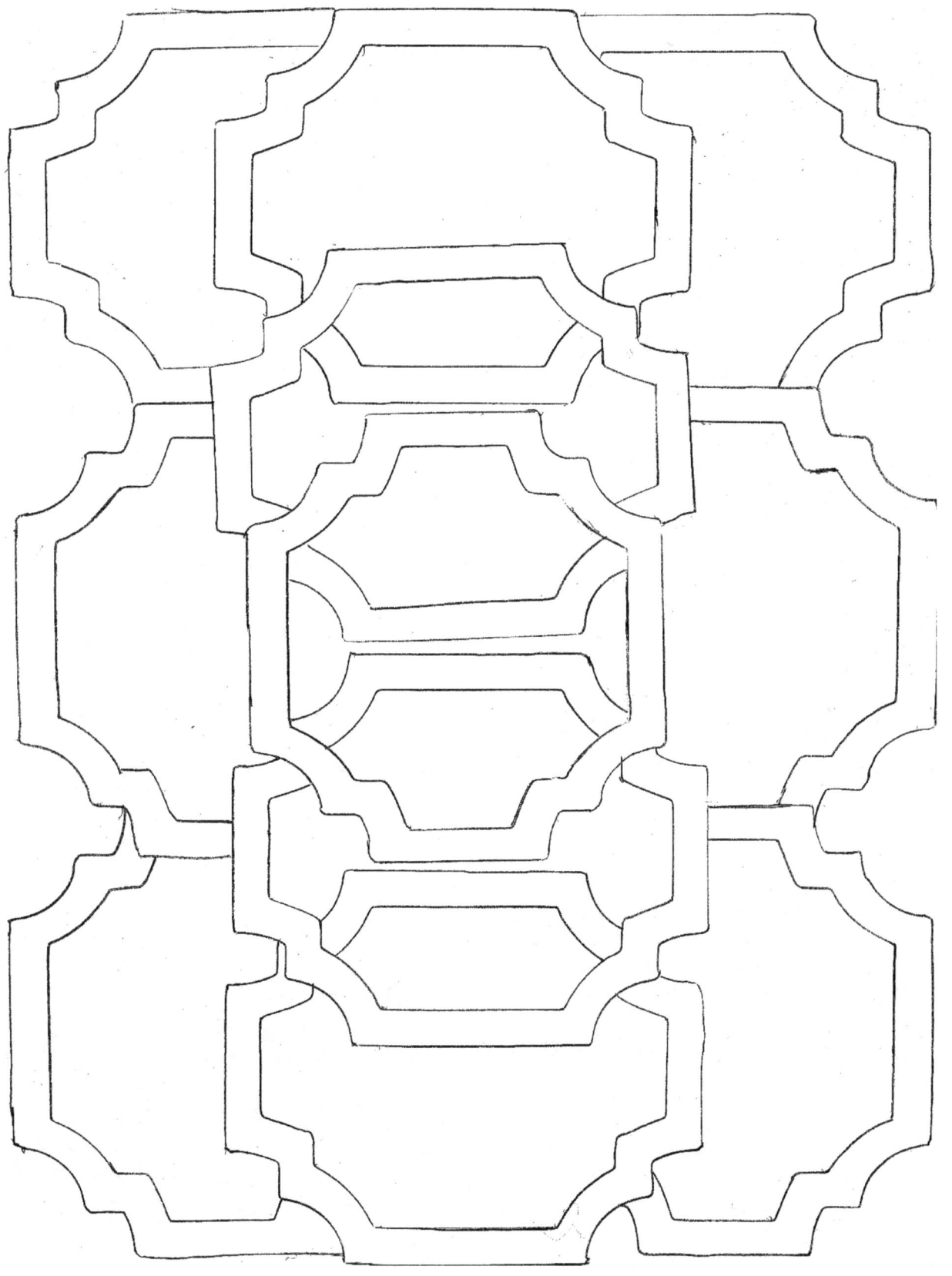

Carol Hopkins

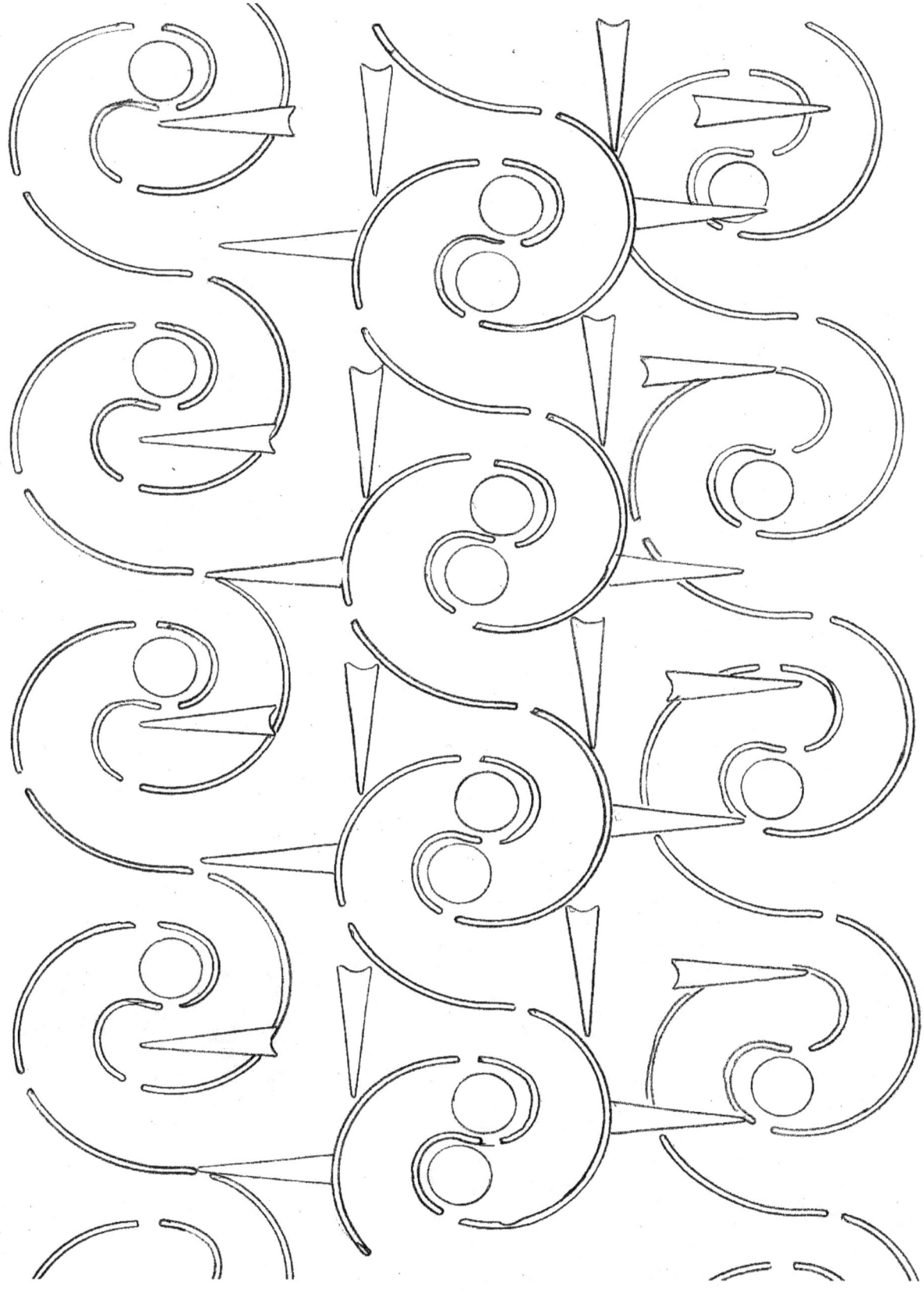

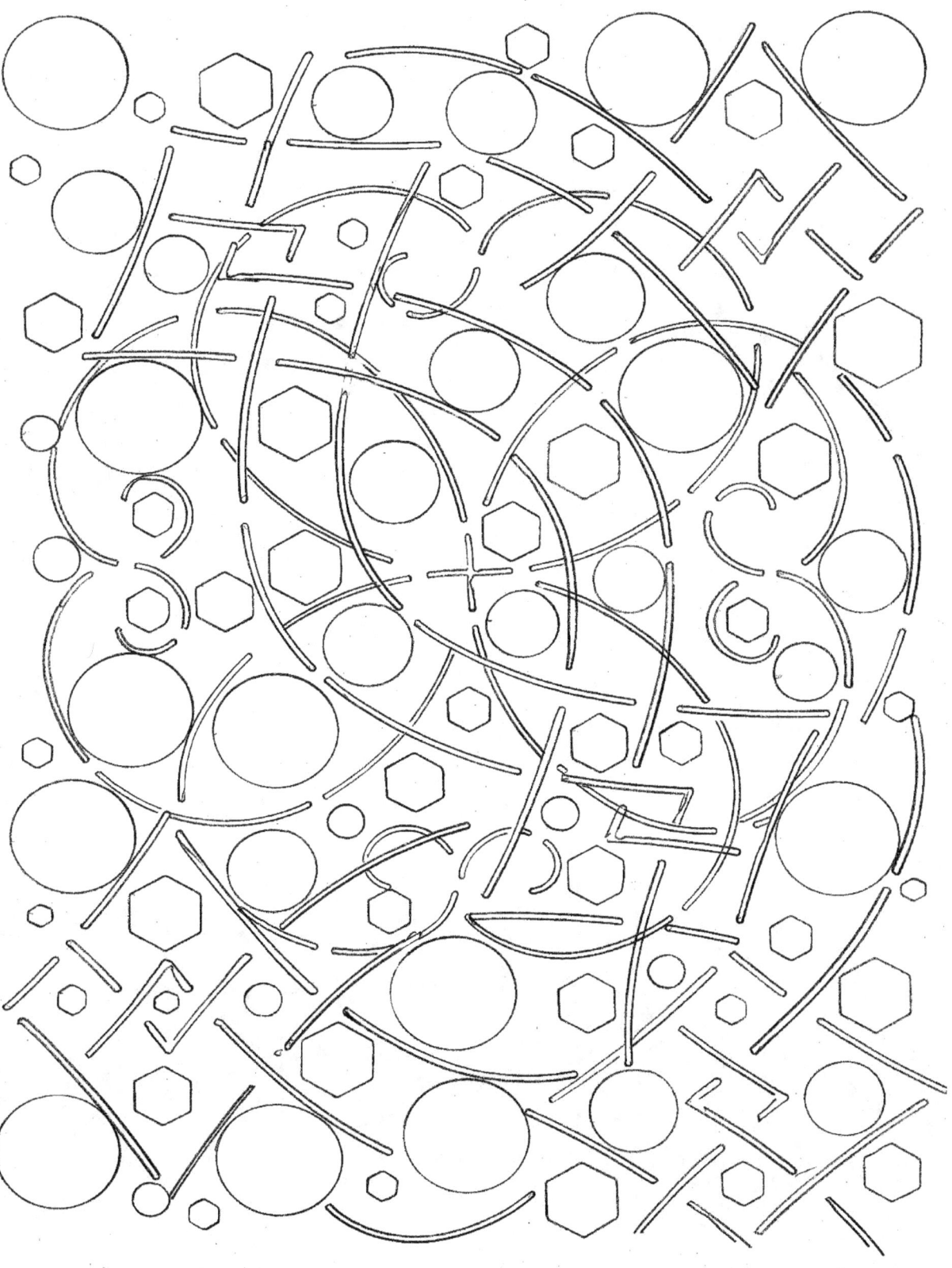

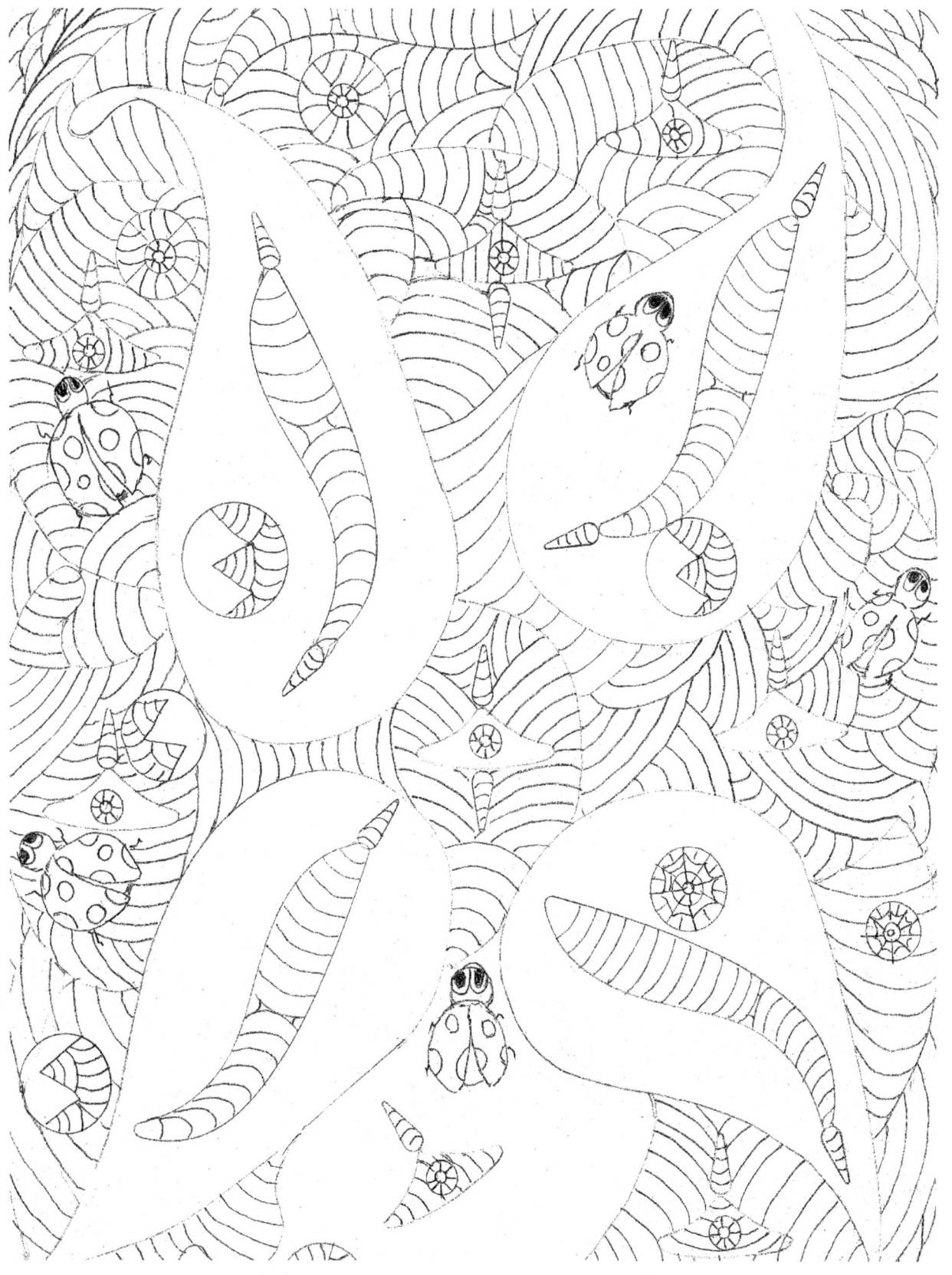

Carol Hopkins

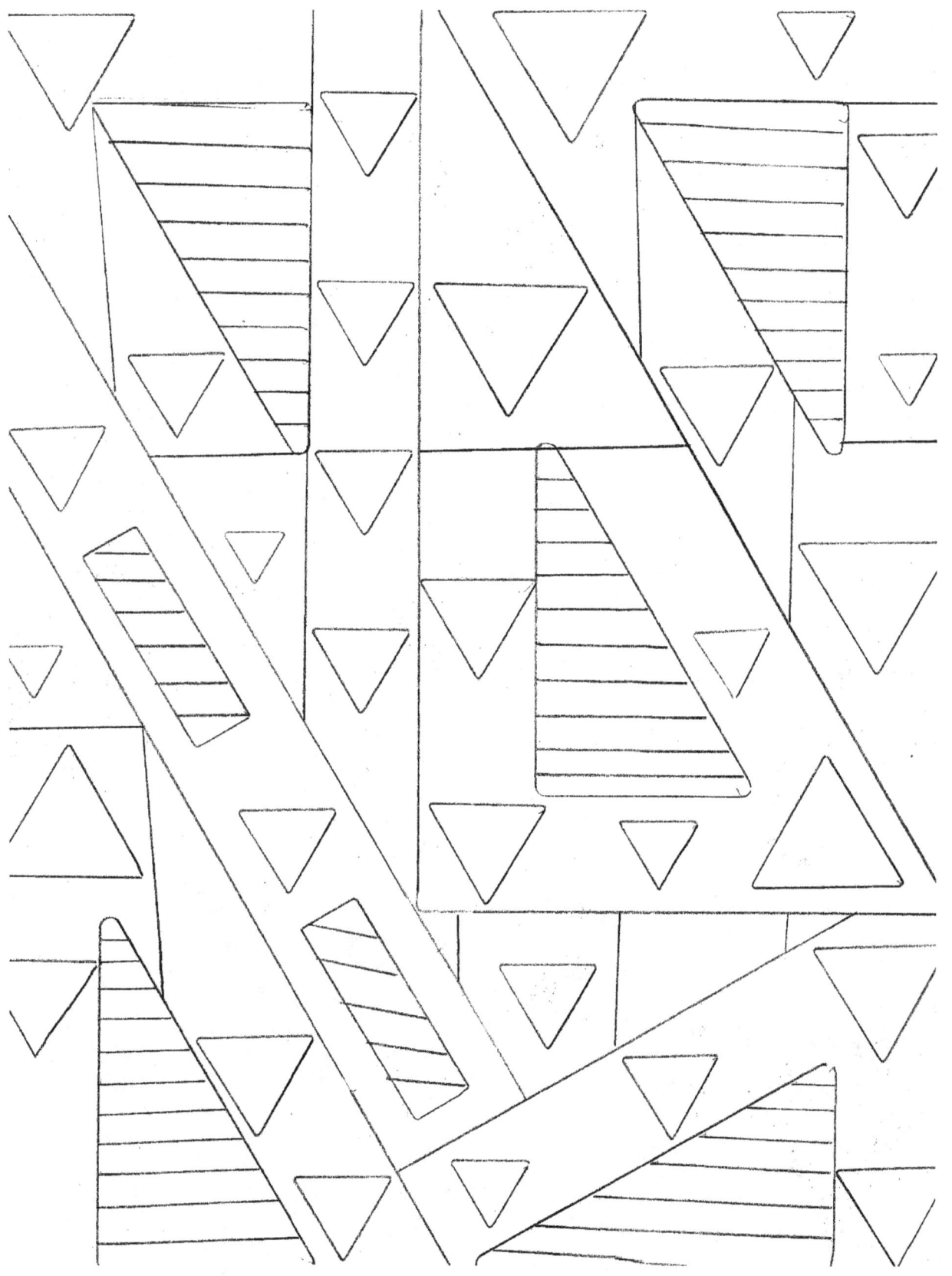

Carol Hopkins

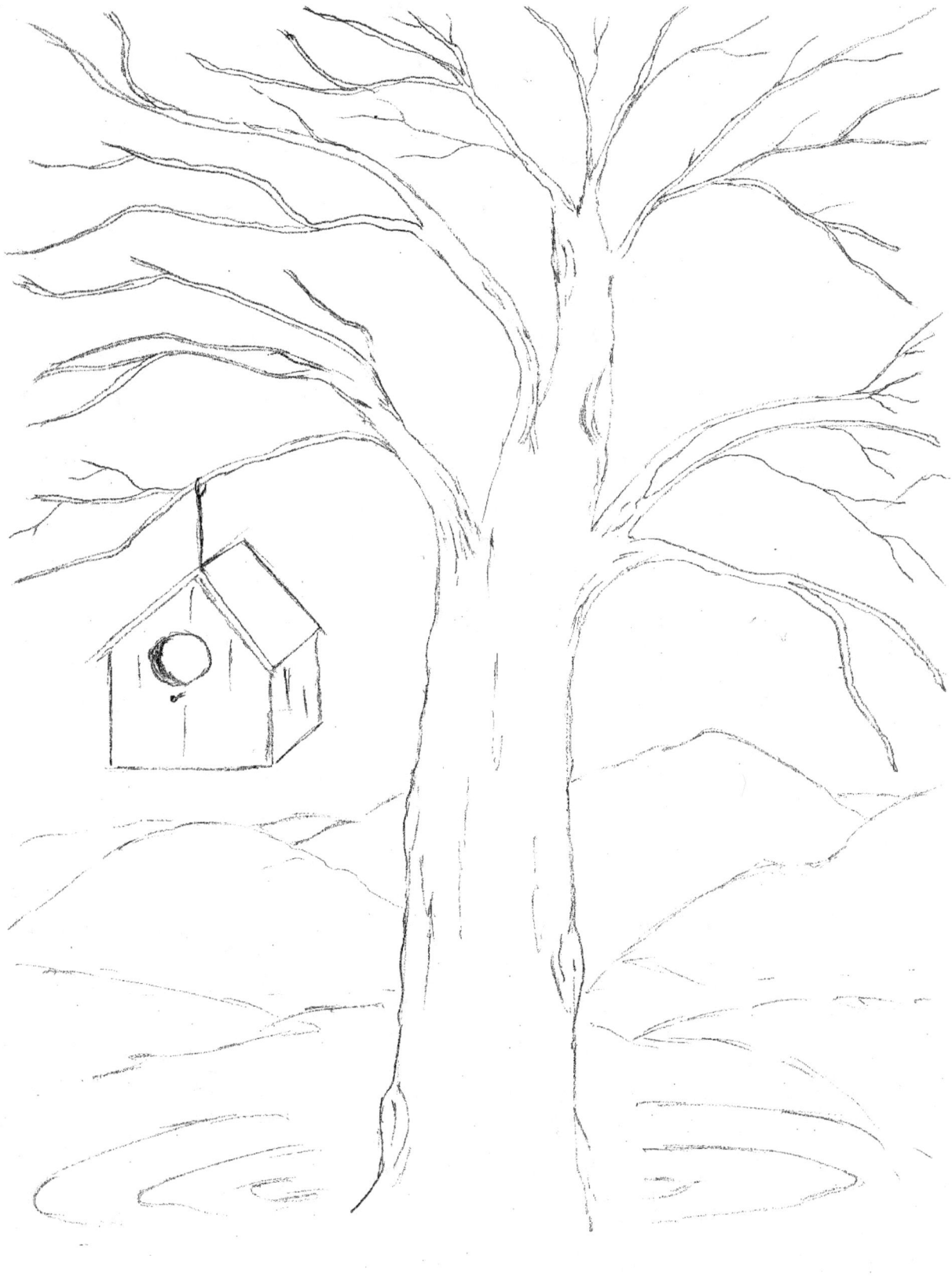

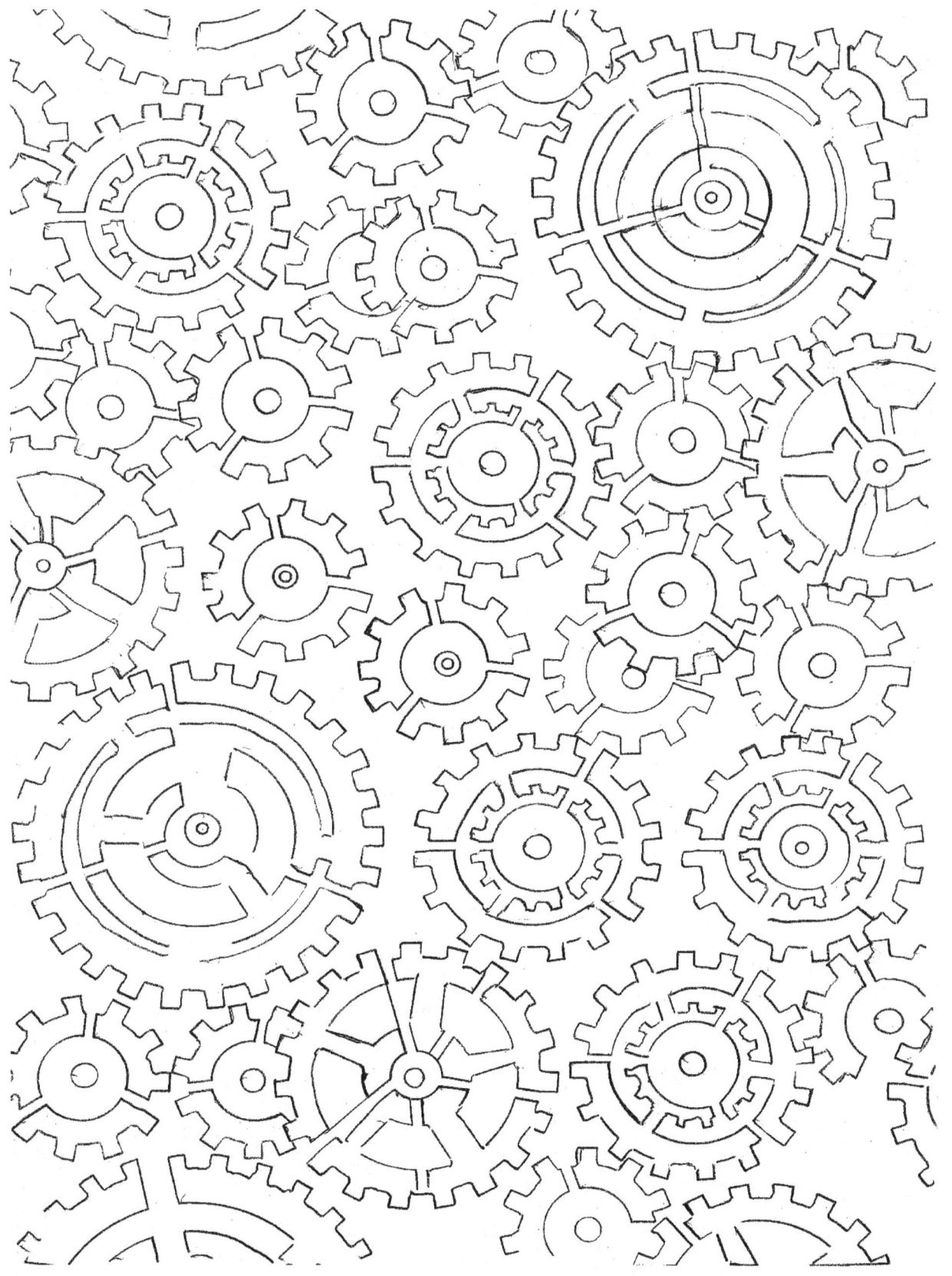

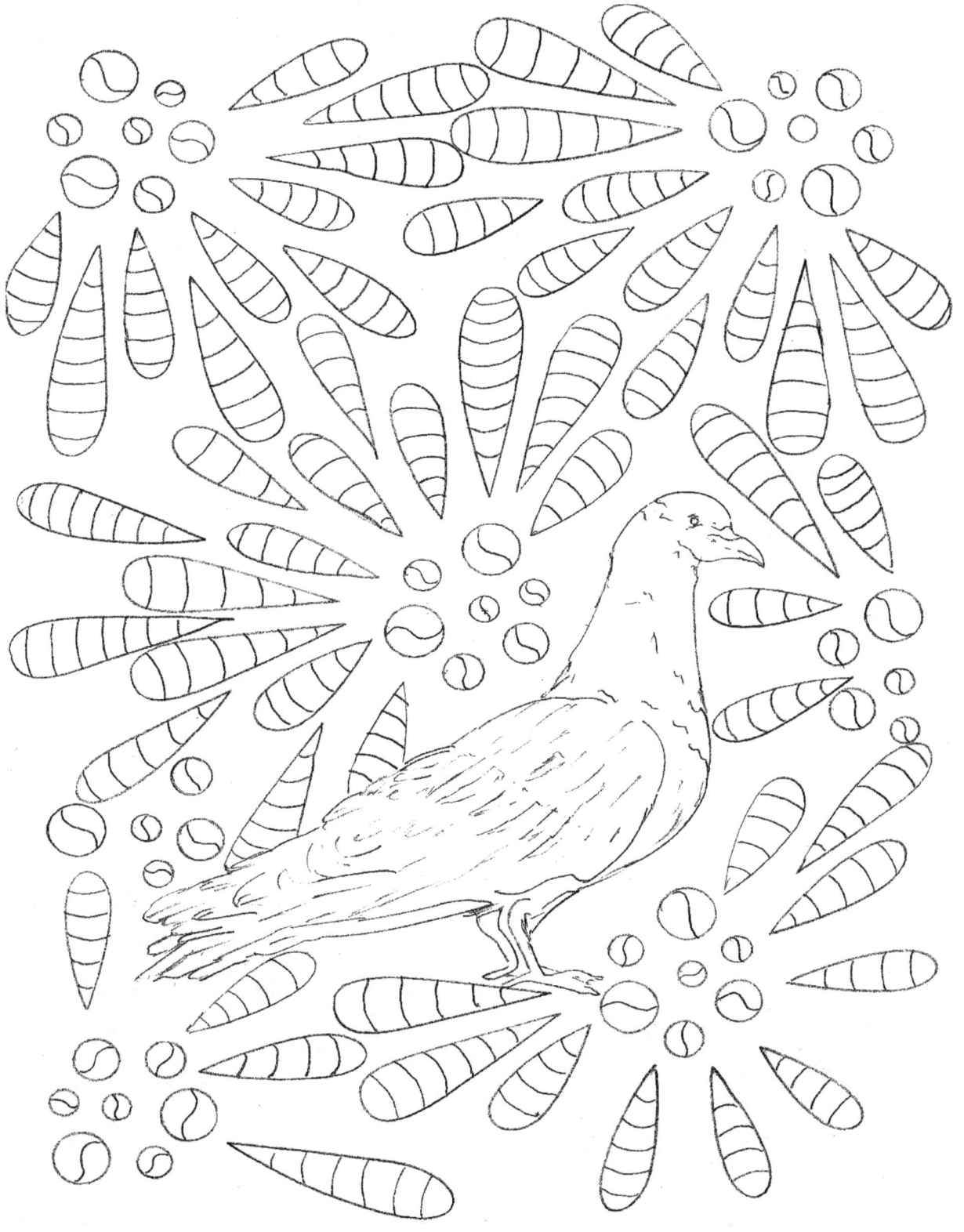

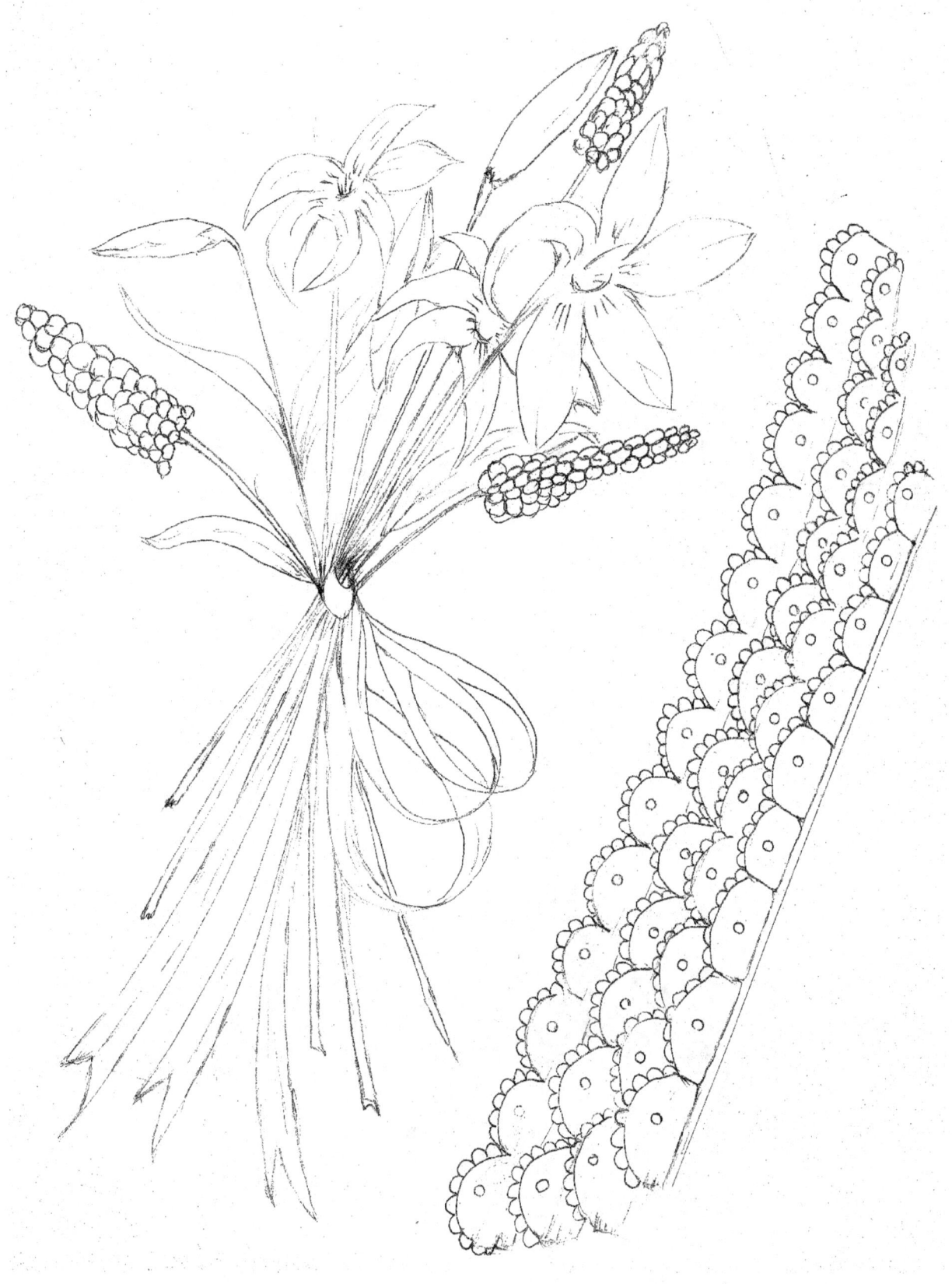

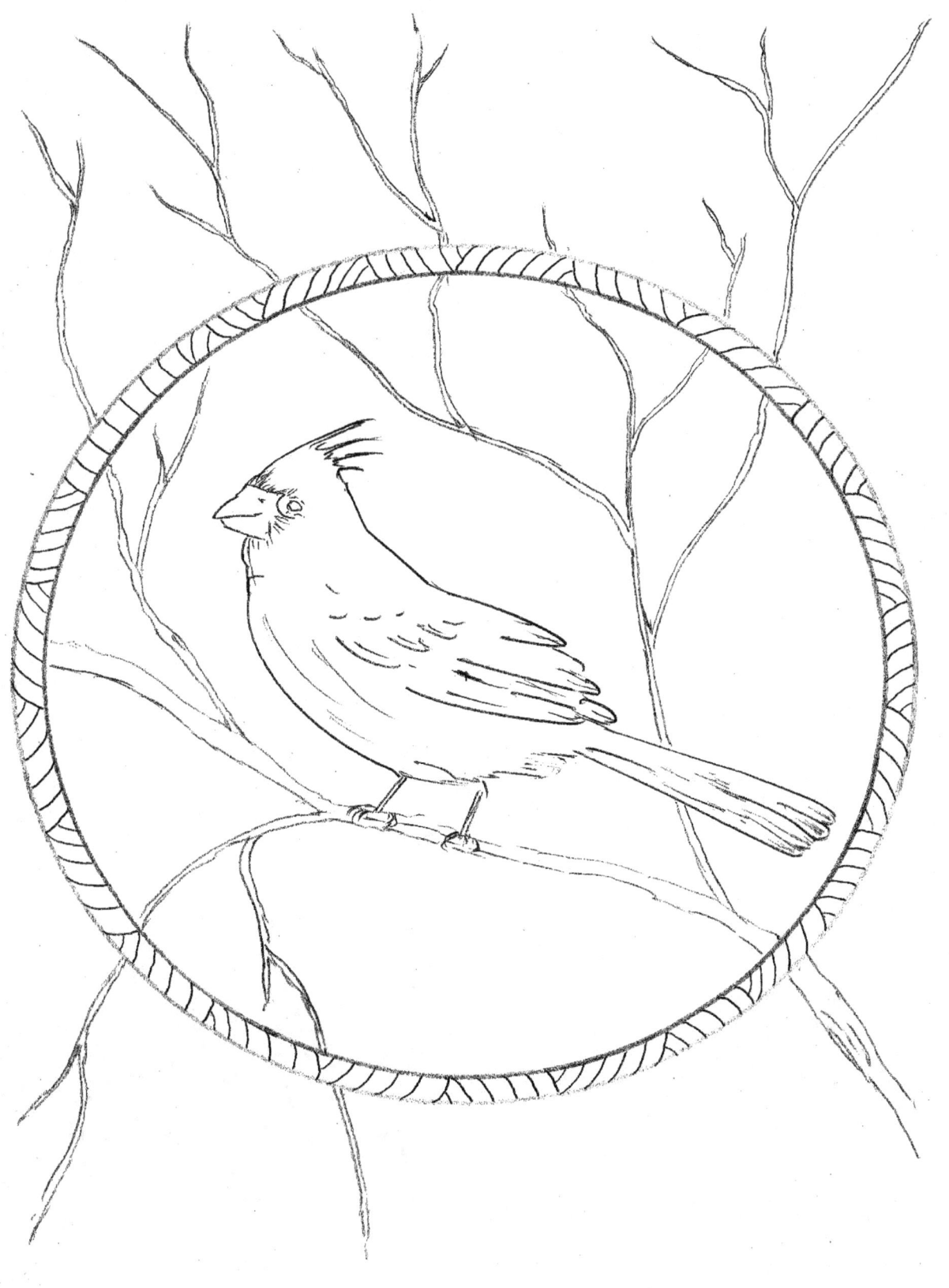

Carol Hopkins

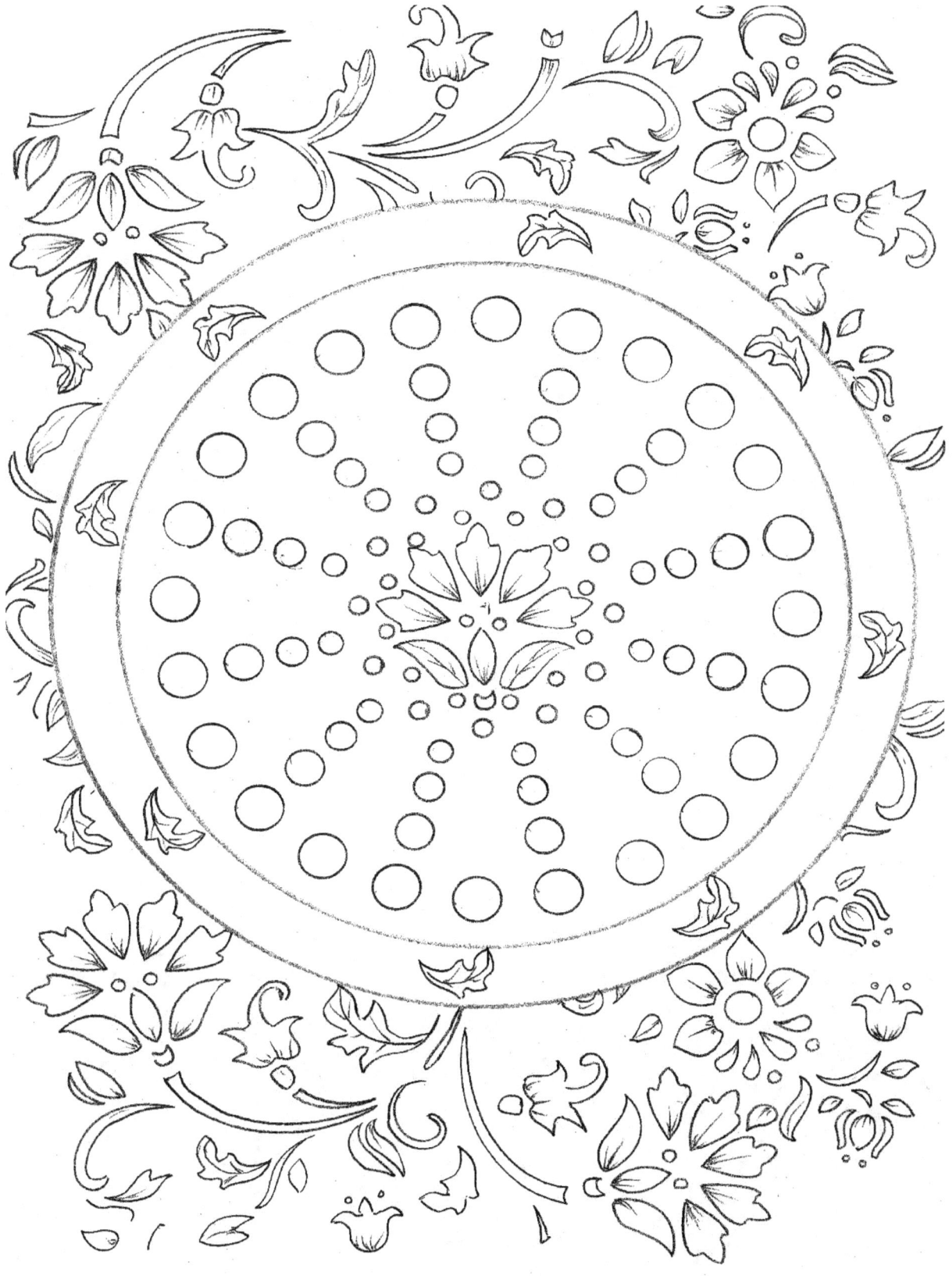

Masks

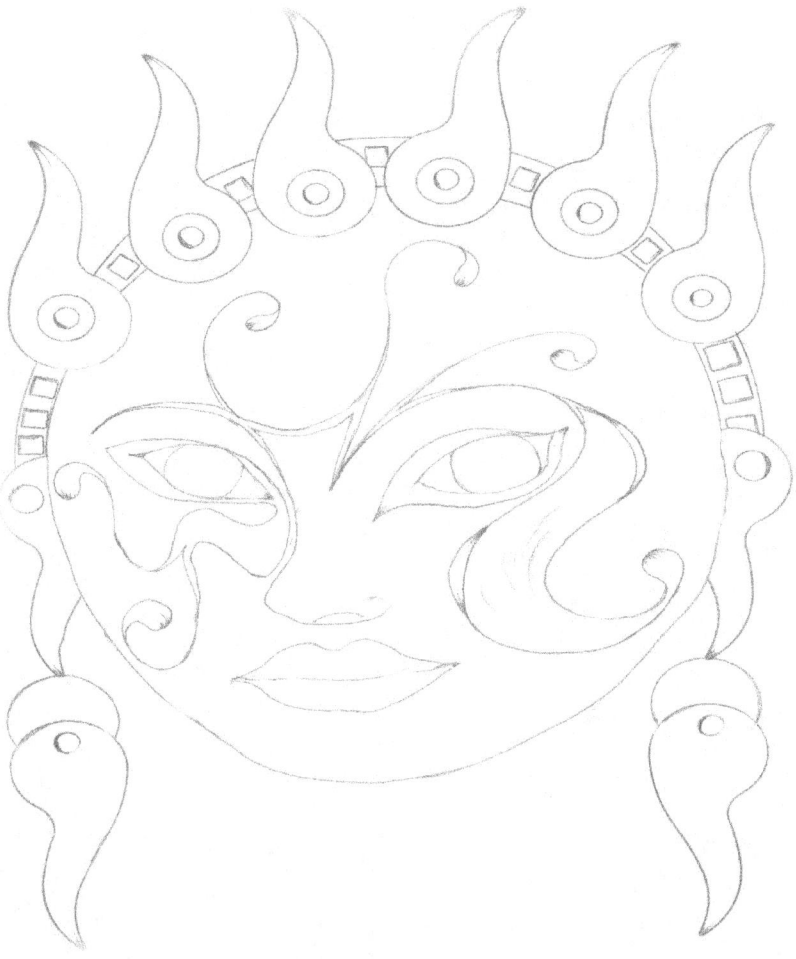

Carol Hopkins

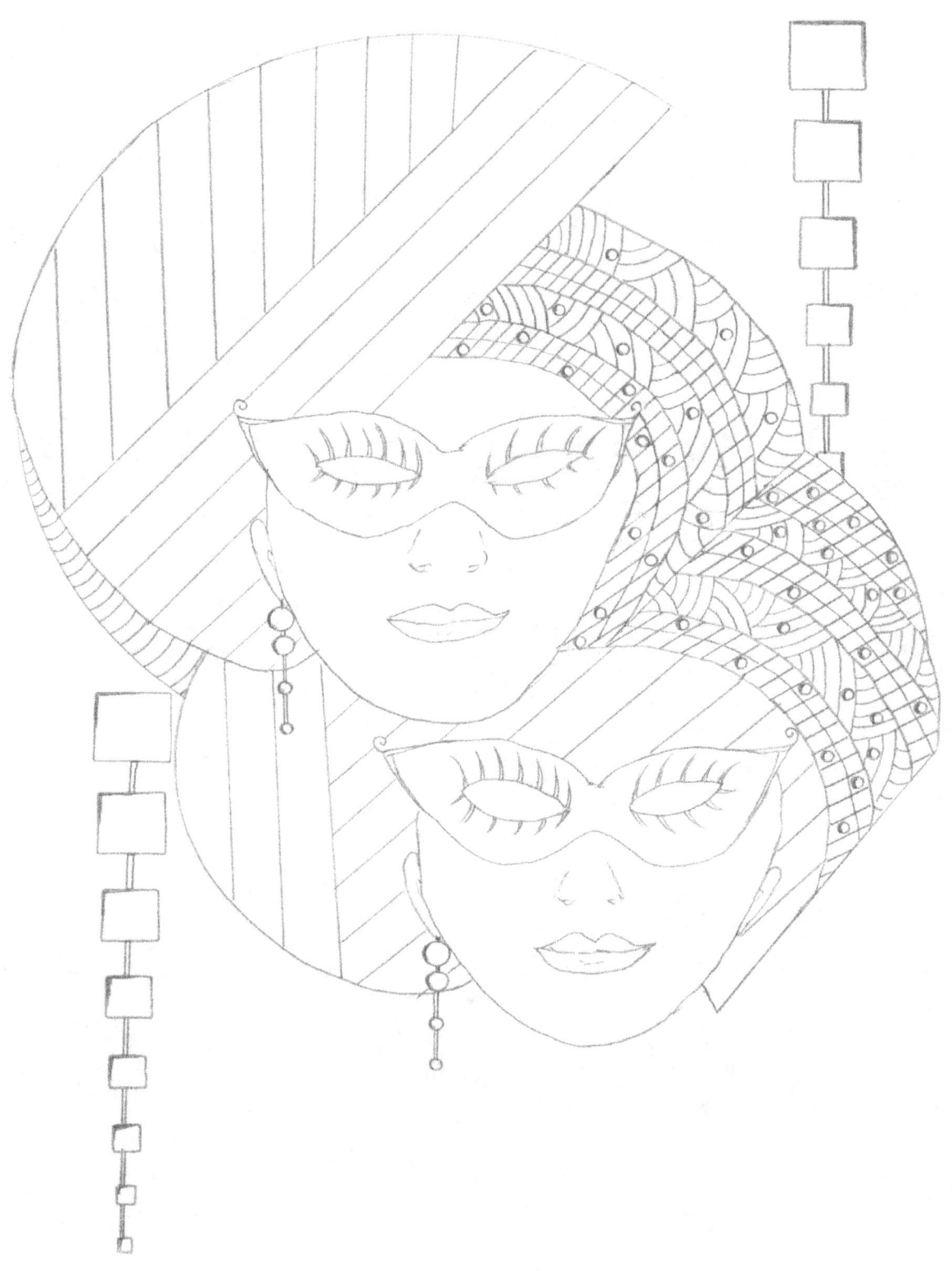

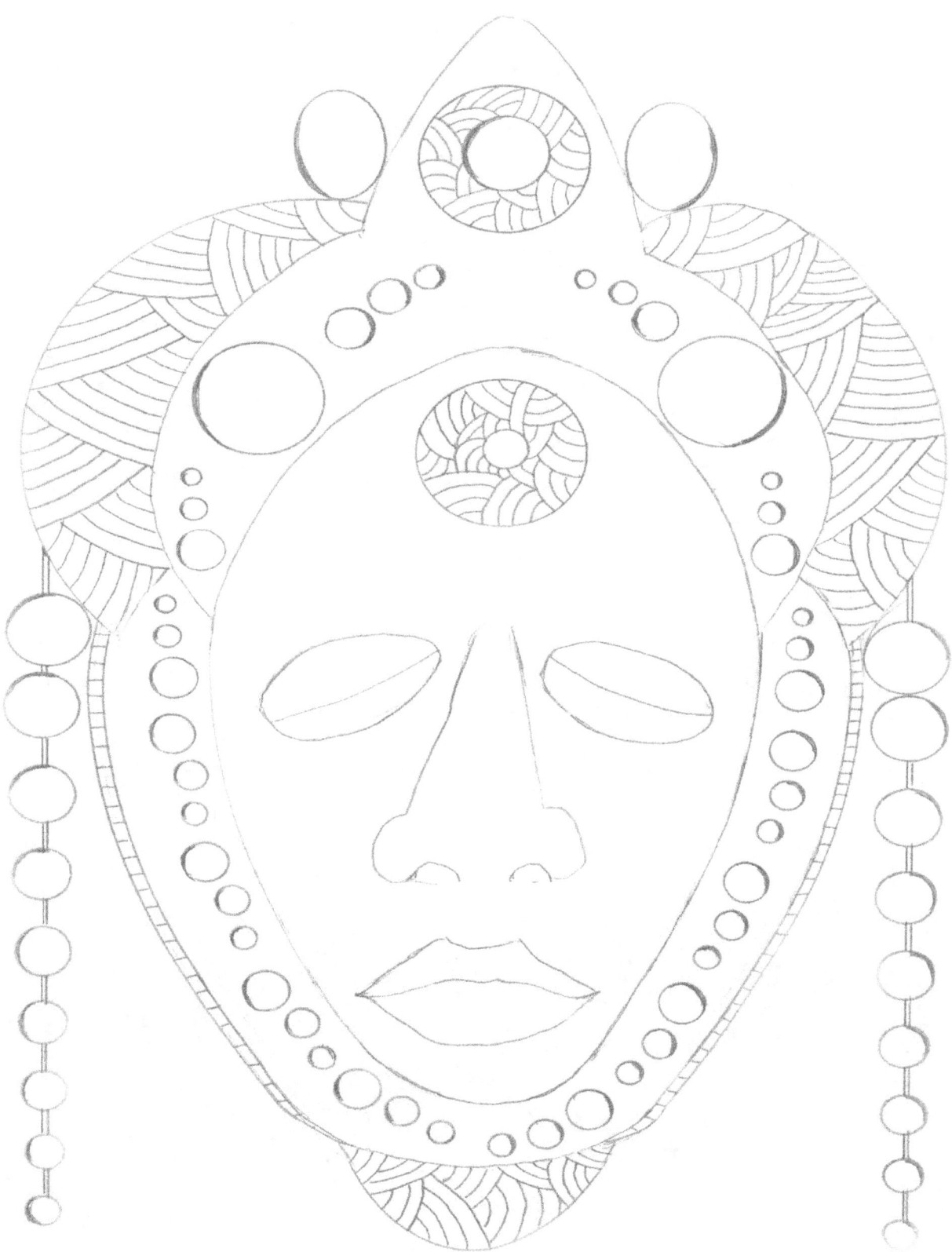

Carol Hopkins

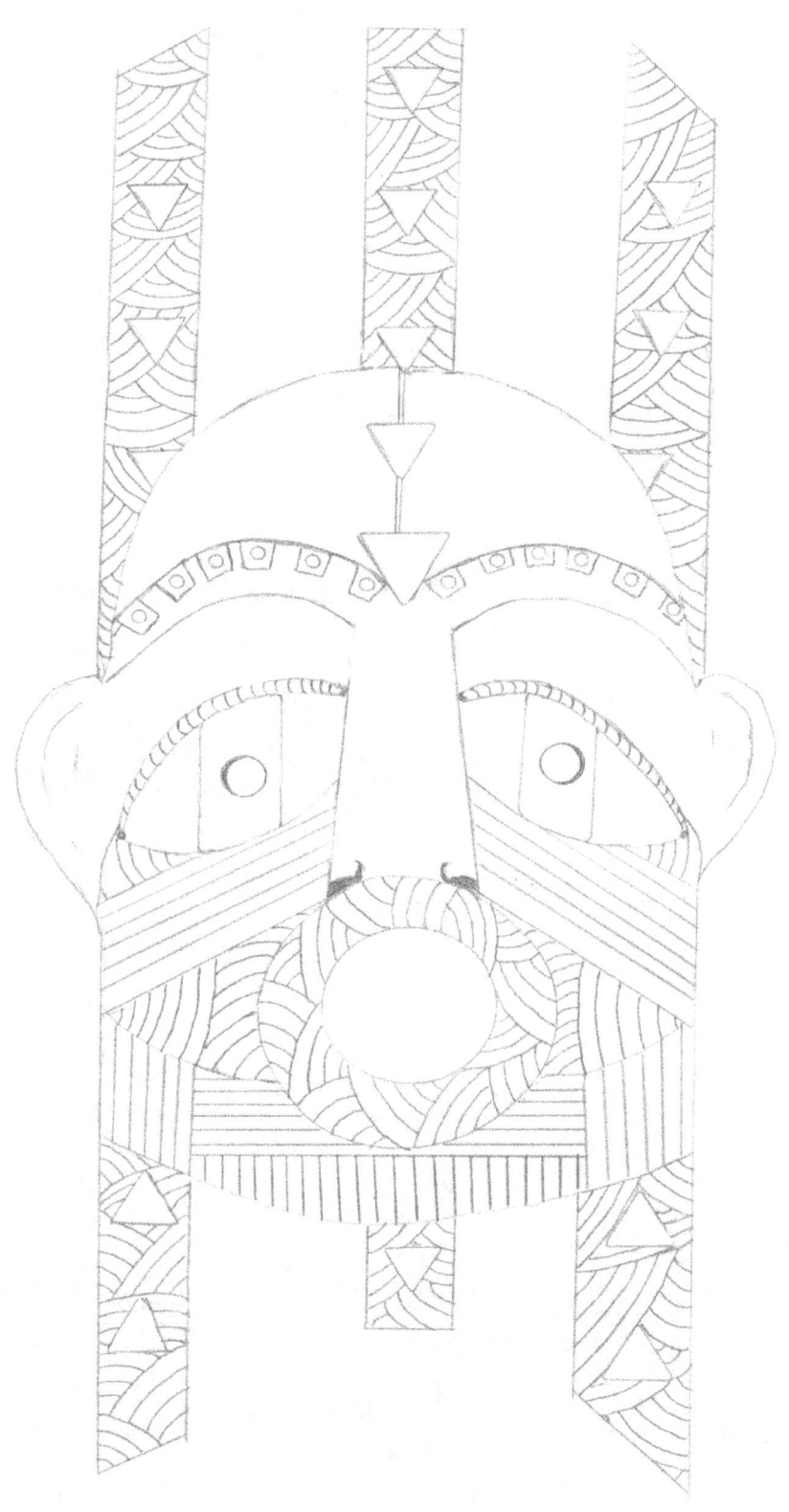

Carol Hopkins

Carol Hopkins

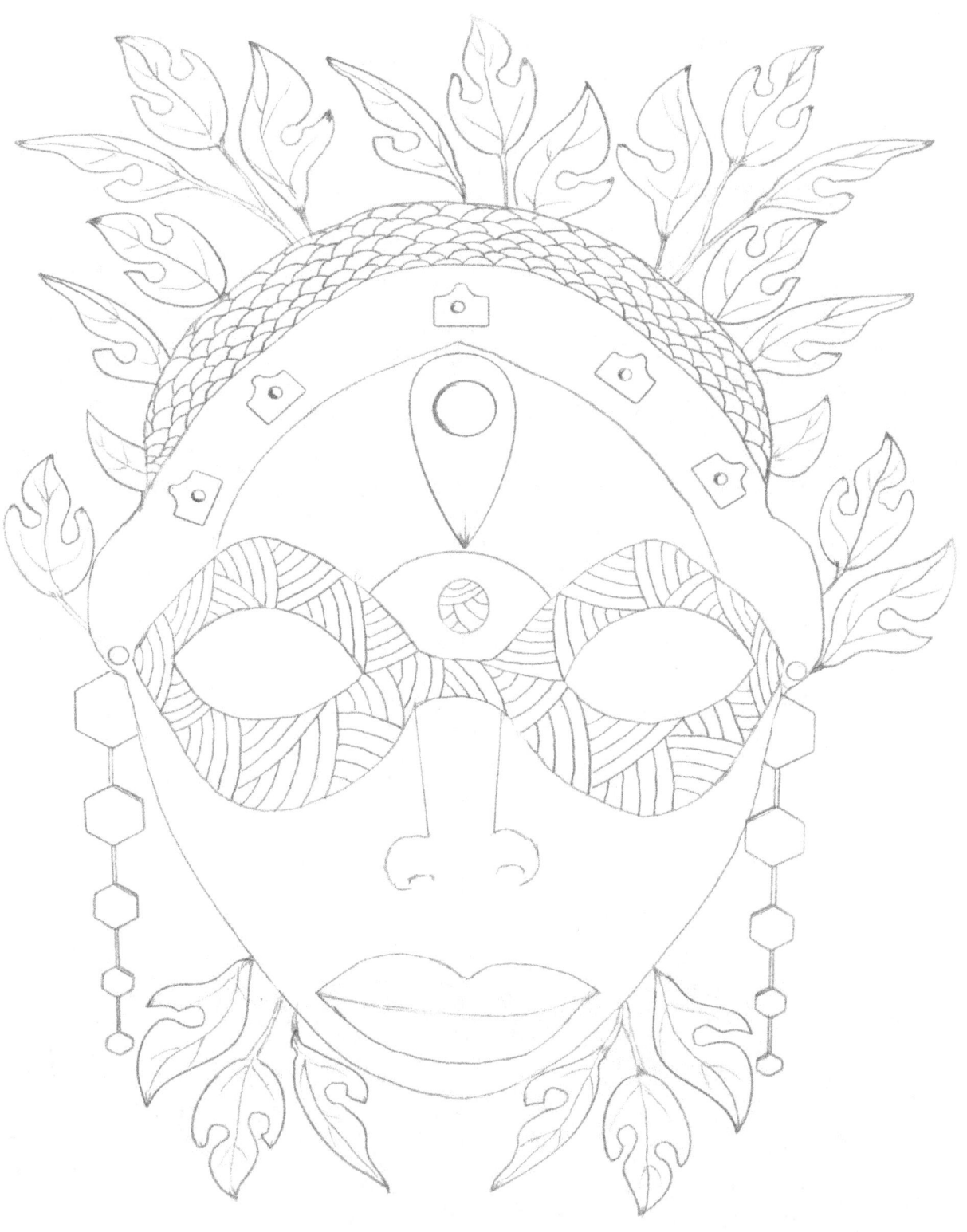

Carol Hopkins

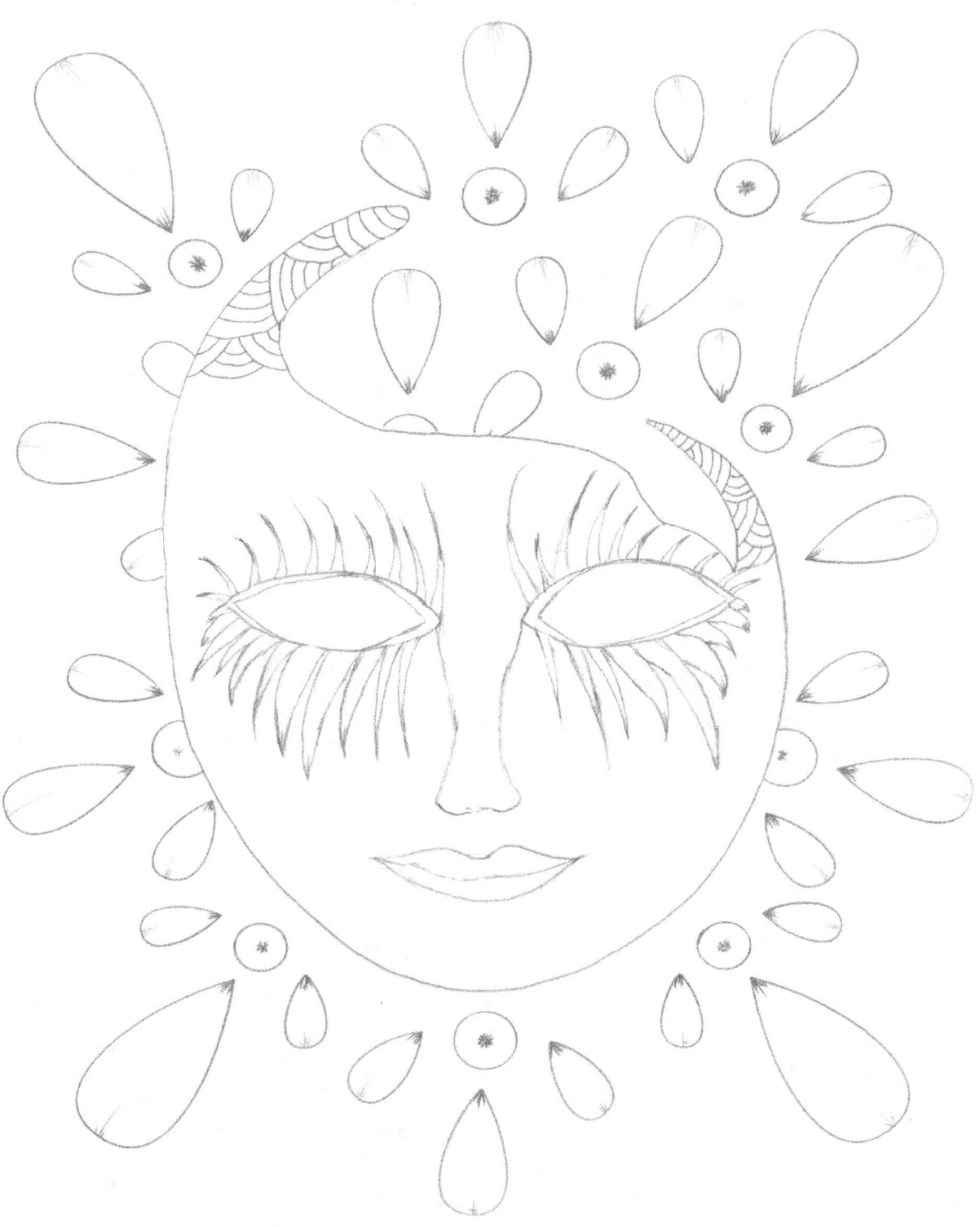

Carol Hopkins

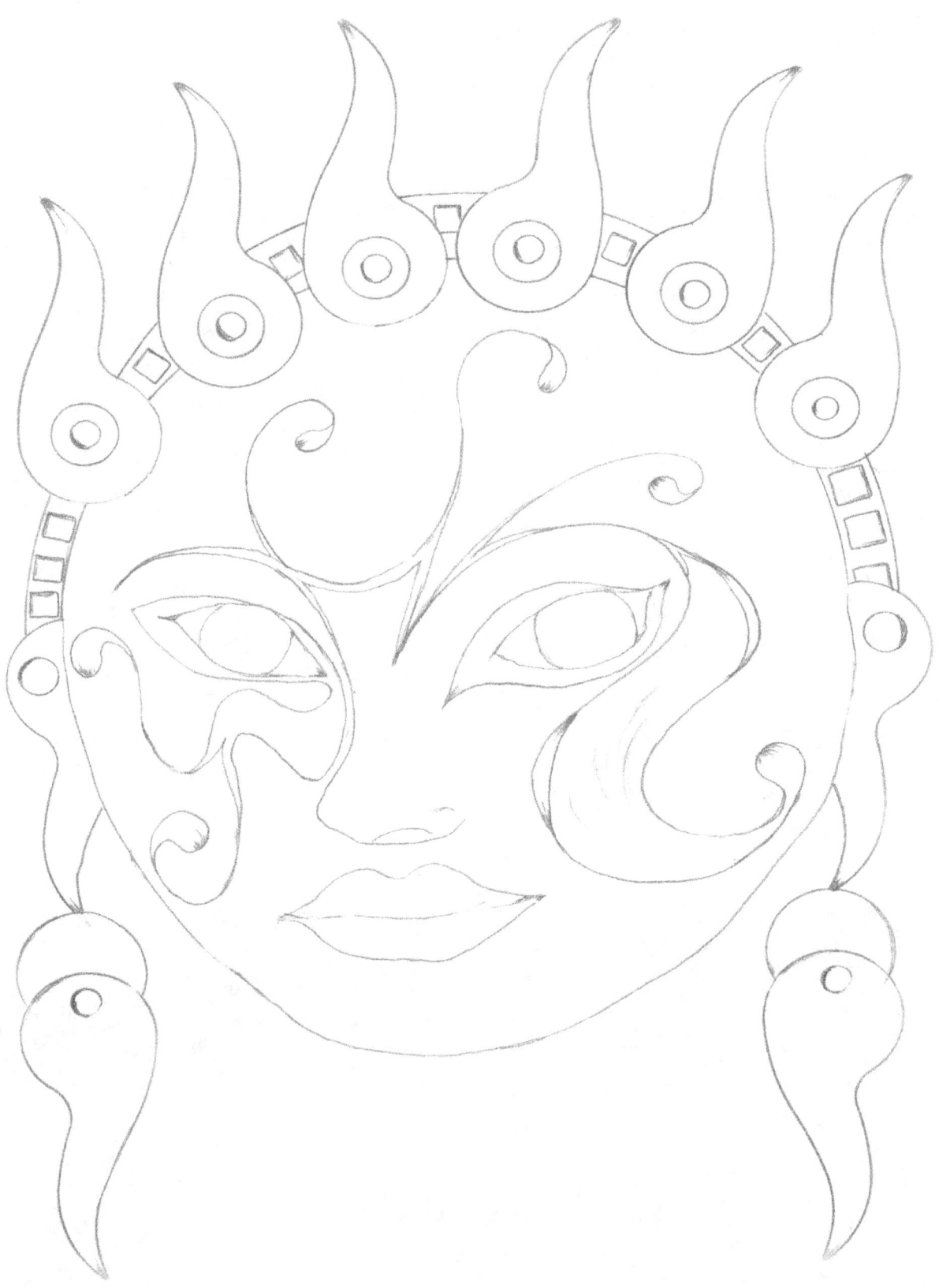

Carol Hopkins

Carol Hopkins

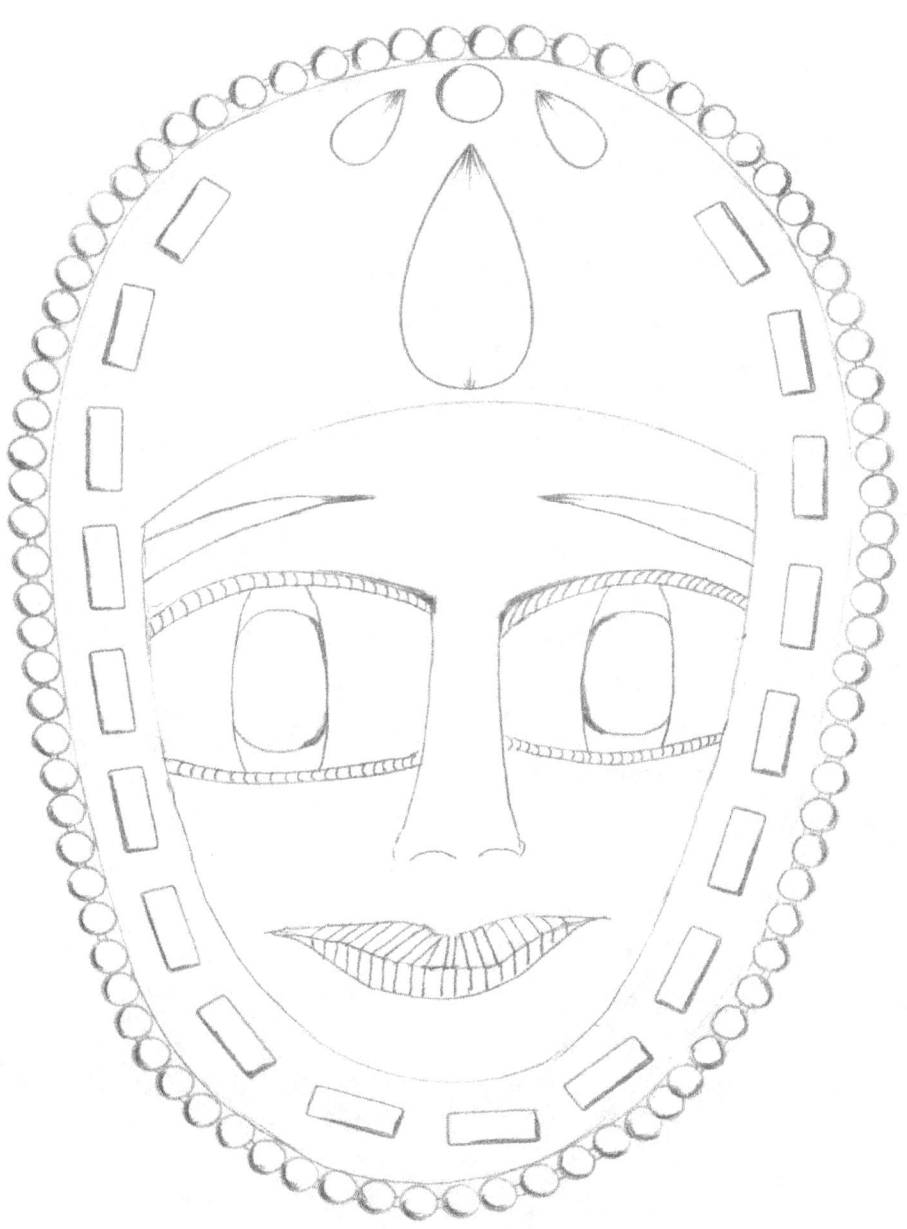

Carol Hopkins

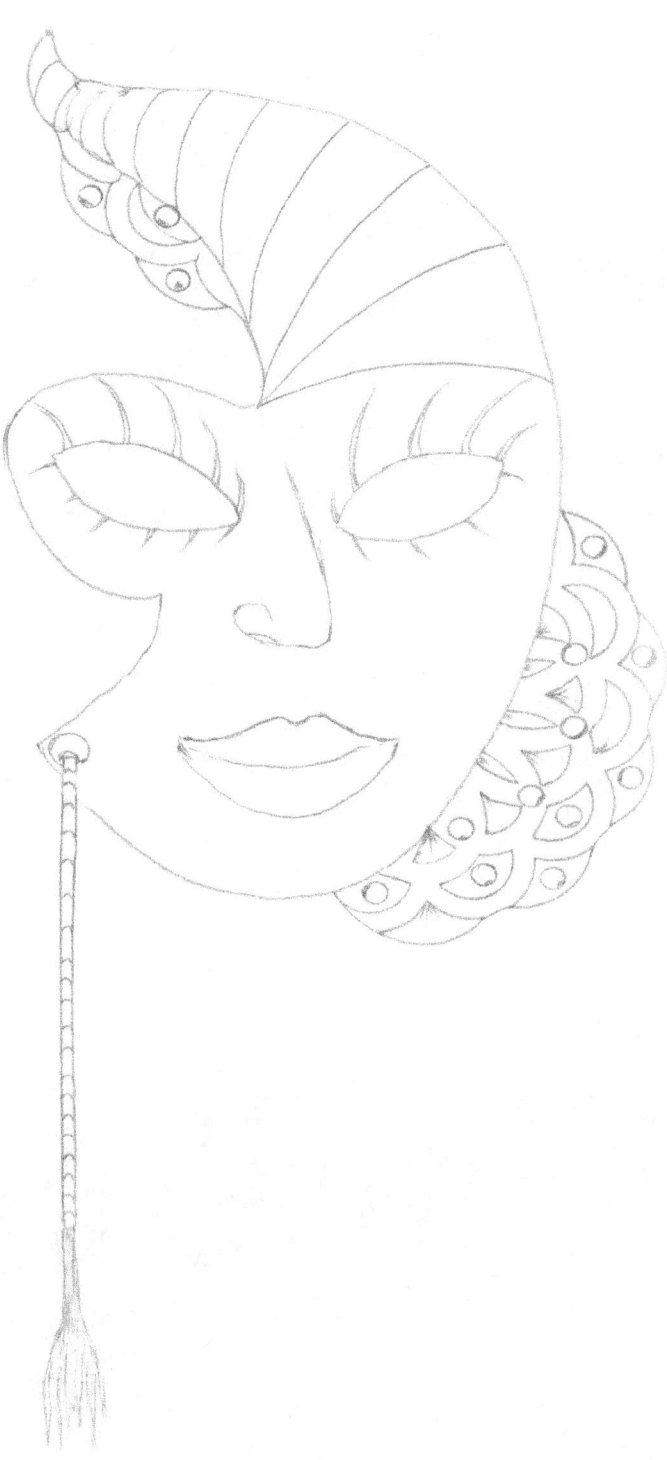

Carol Hopkins

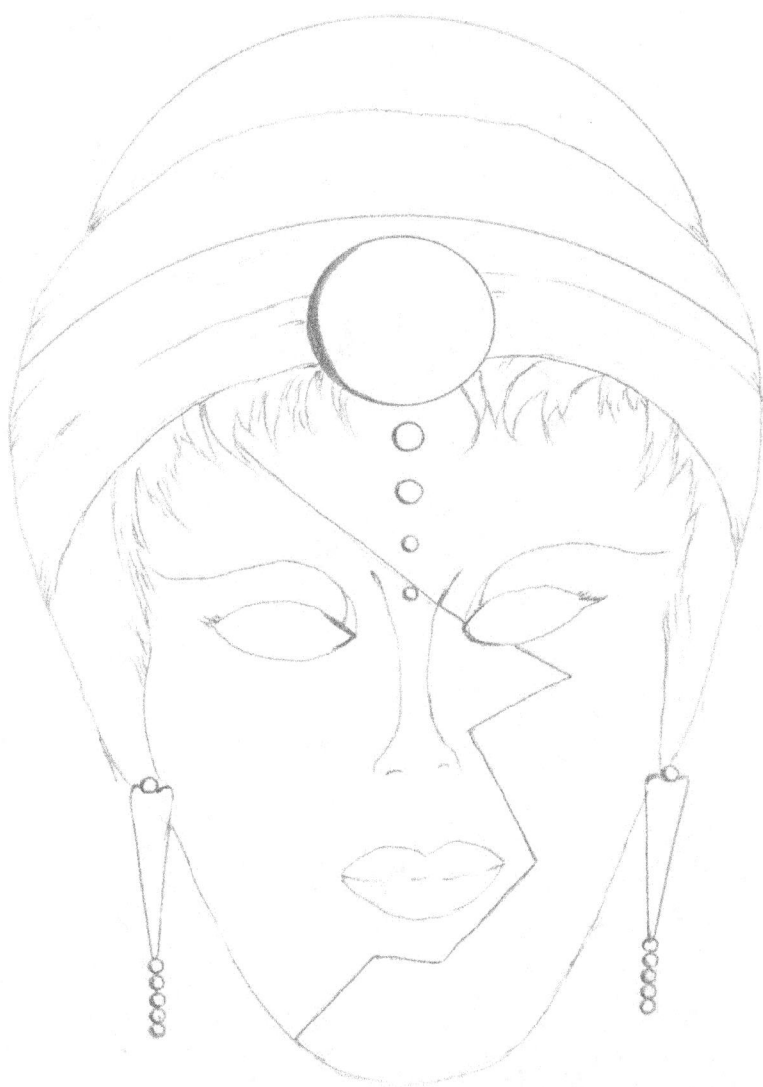

Carol Hopkins

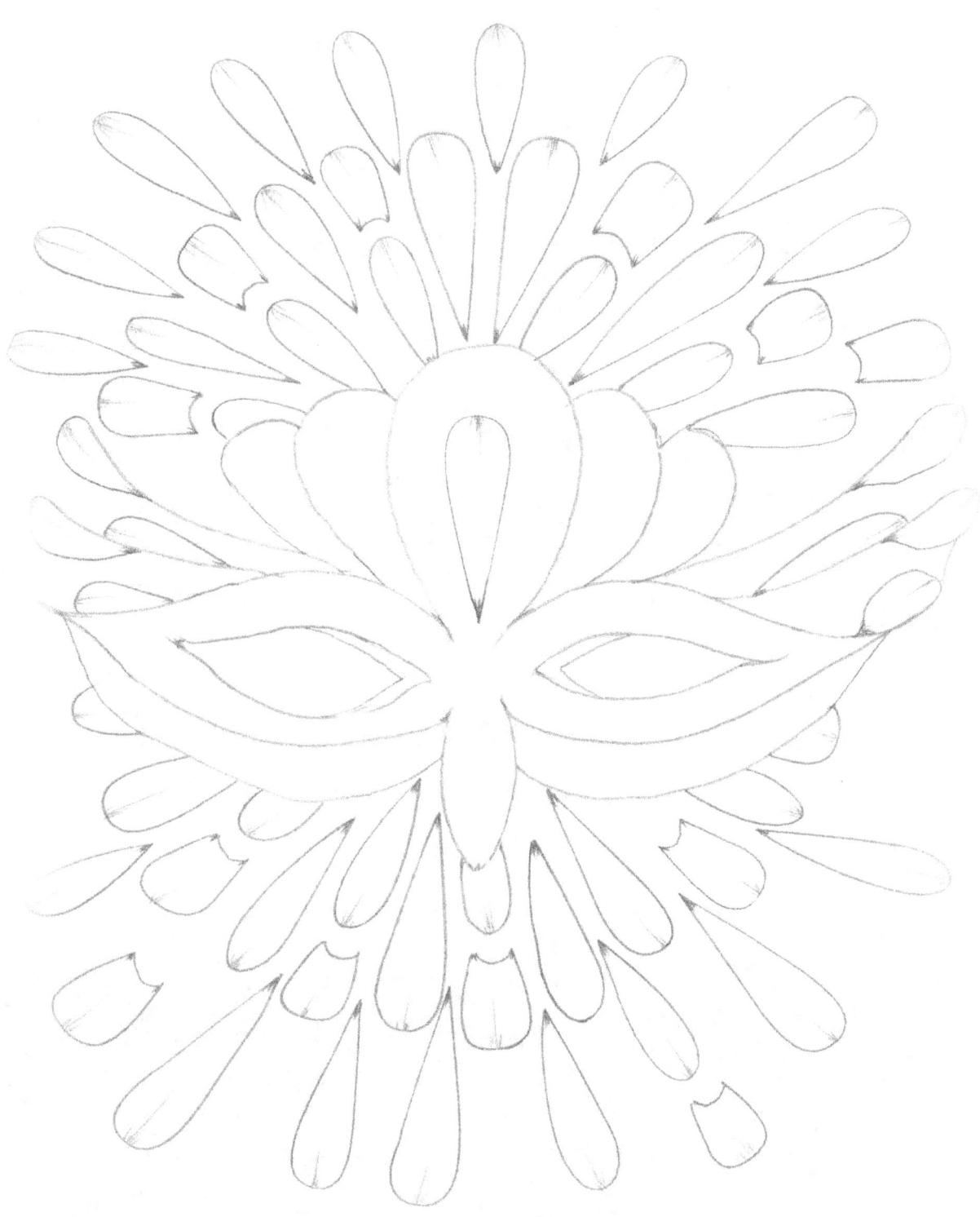

Carol Hopkins

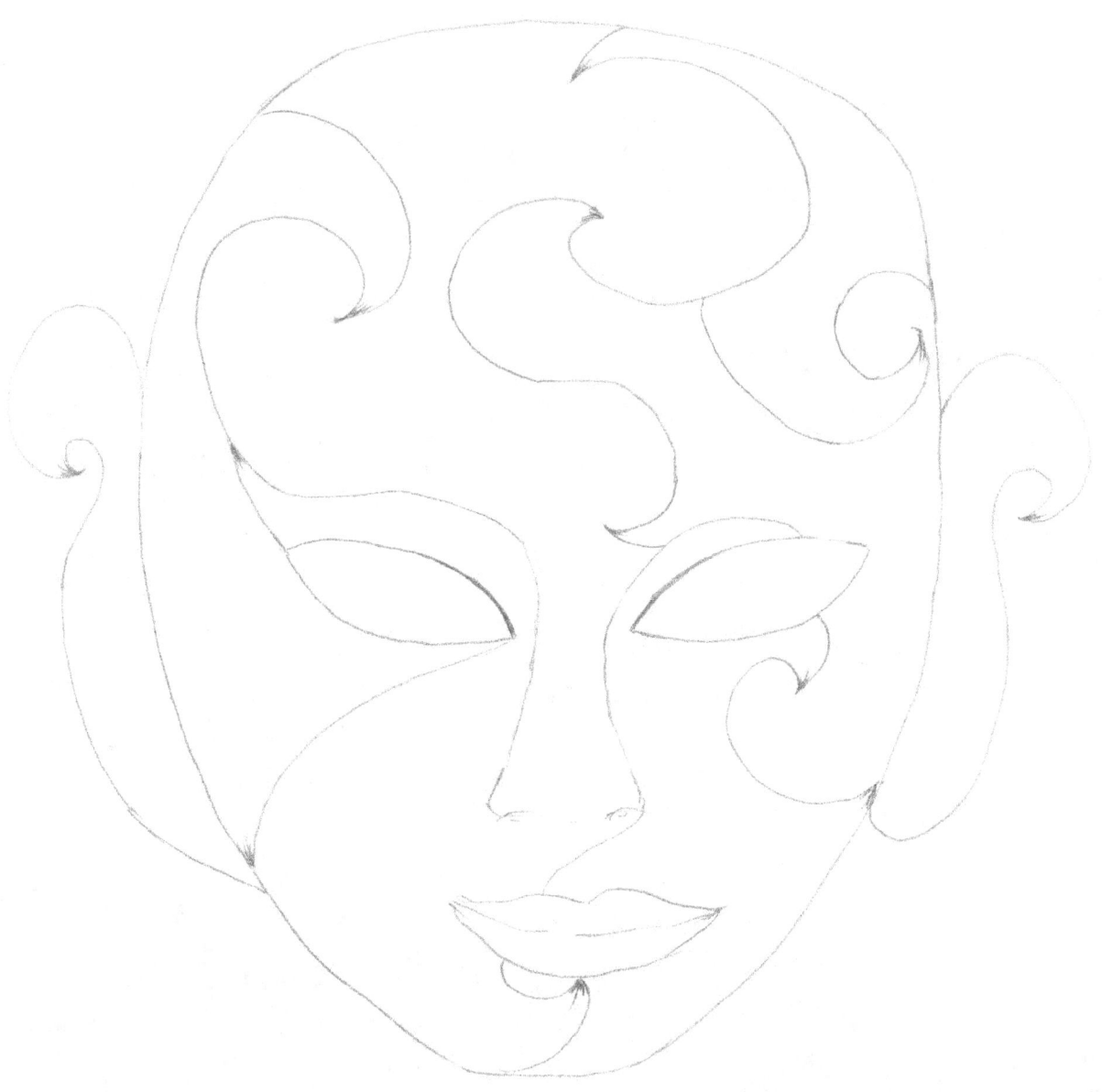

Carol Hopkins

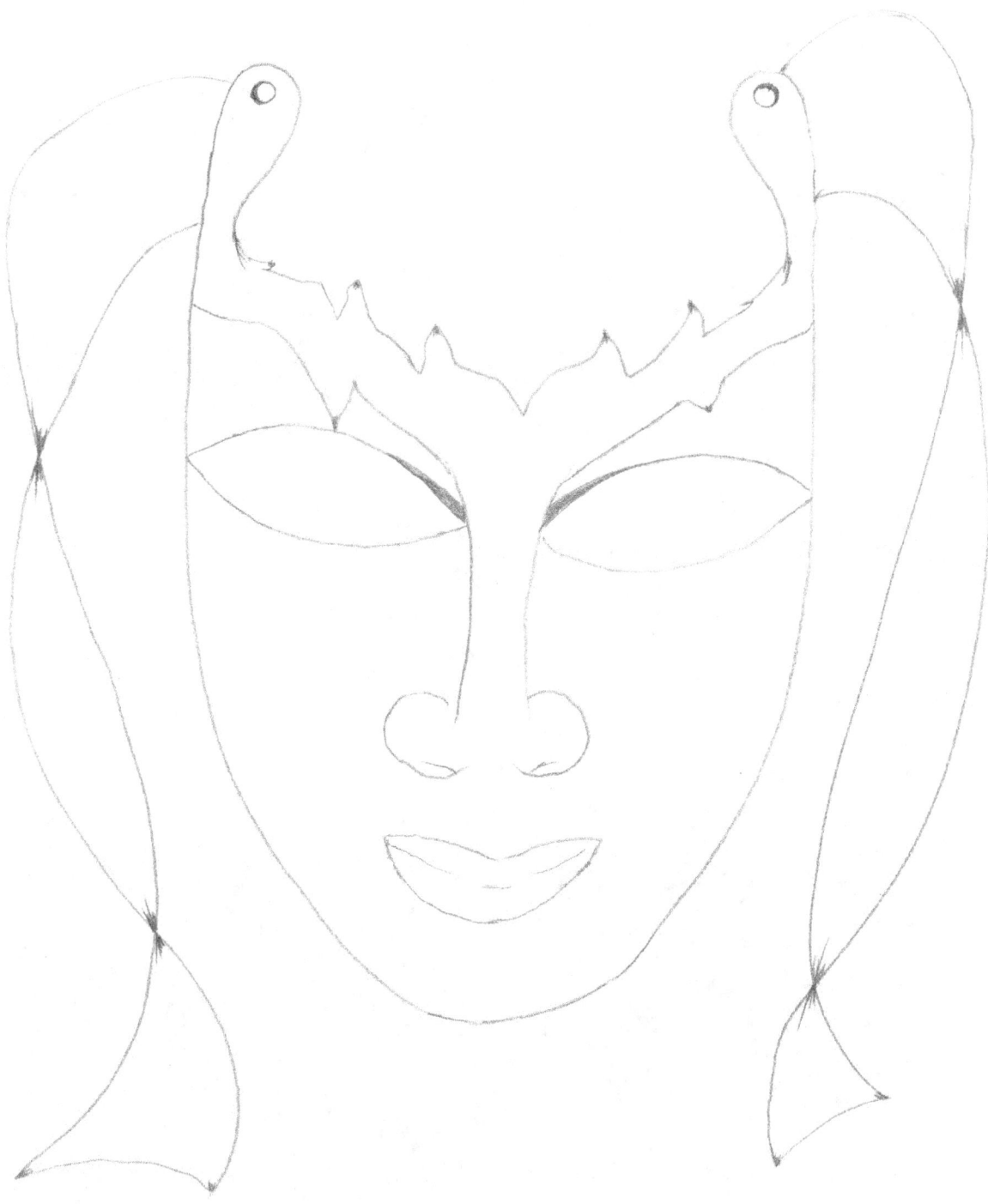

Carol Hopkins

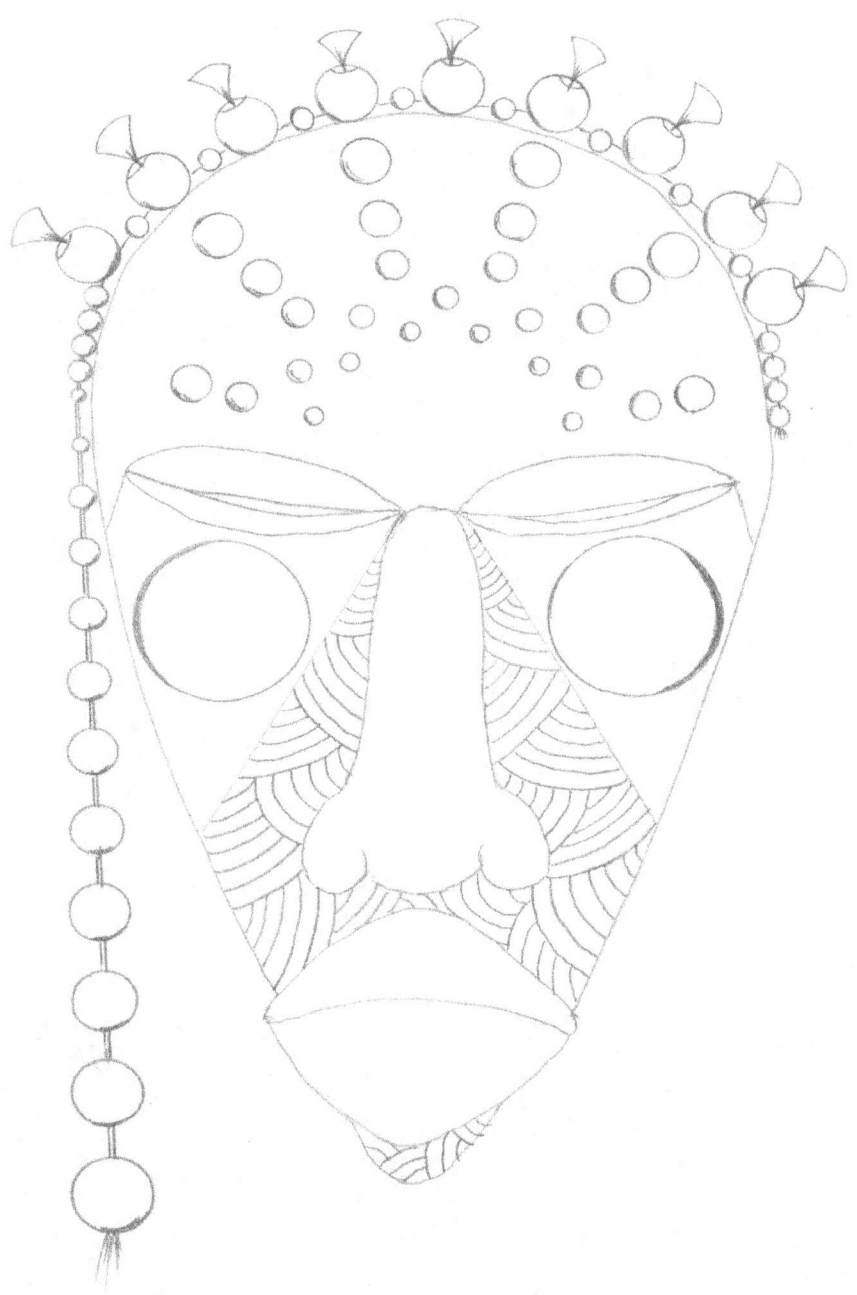

Carol Hopkins

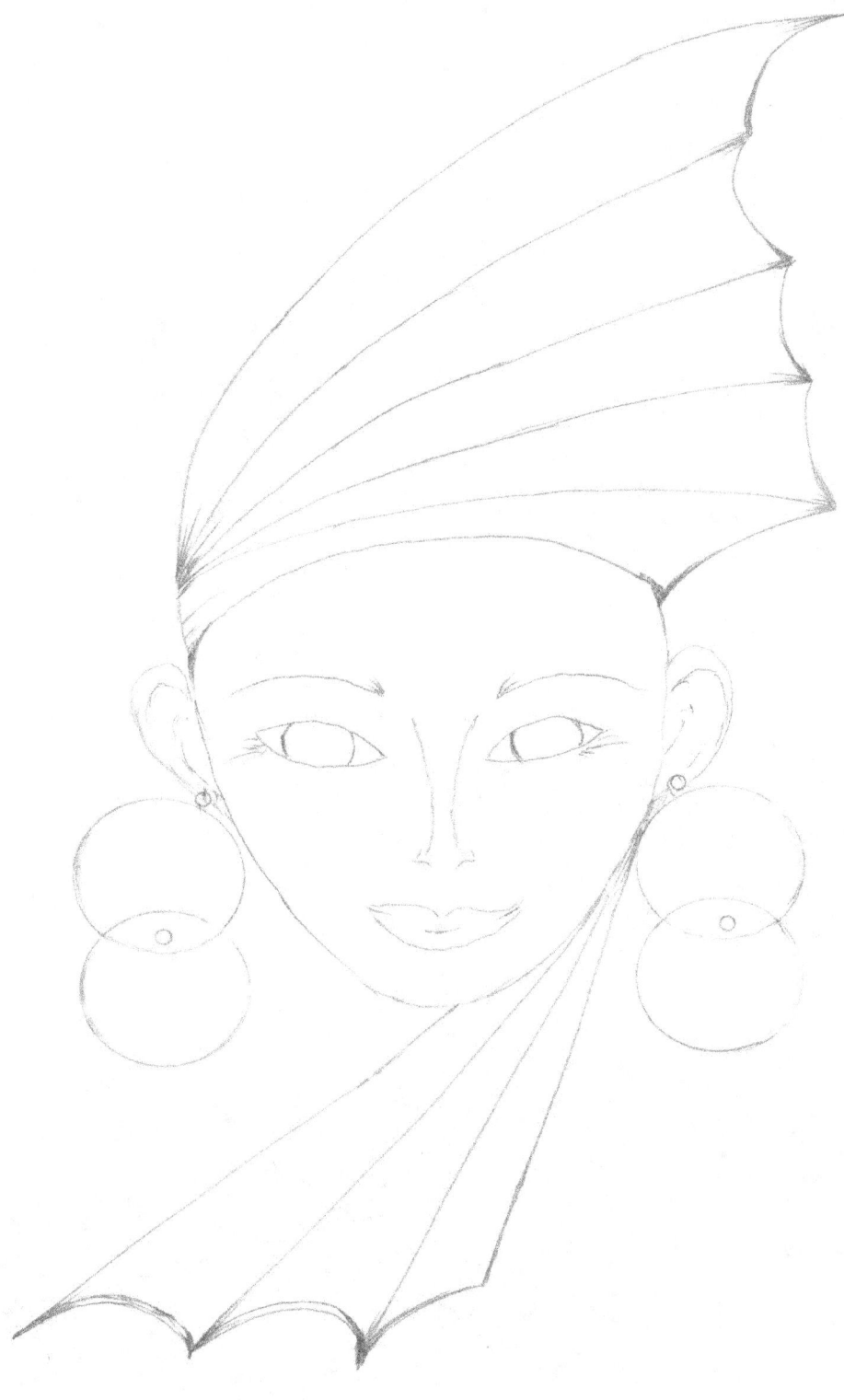

Carol Hopkins

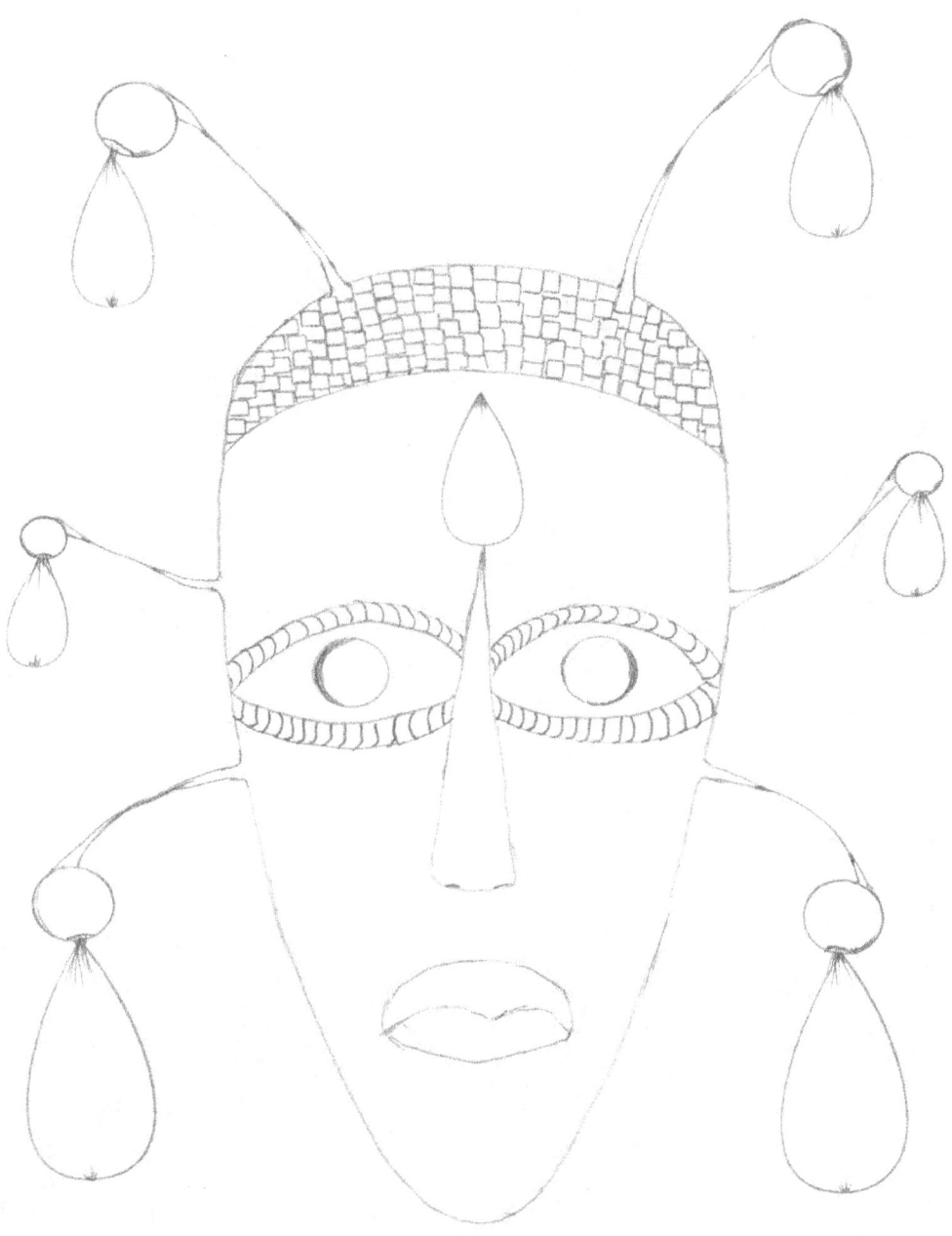

Carol Hopkins

Carol Hopkins

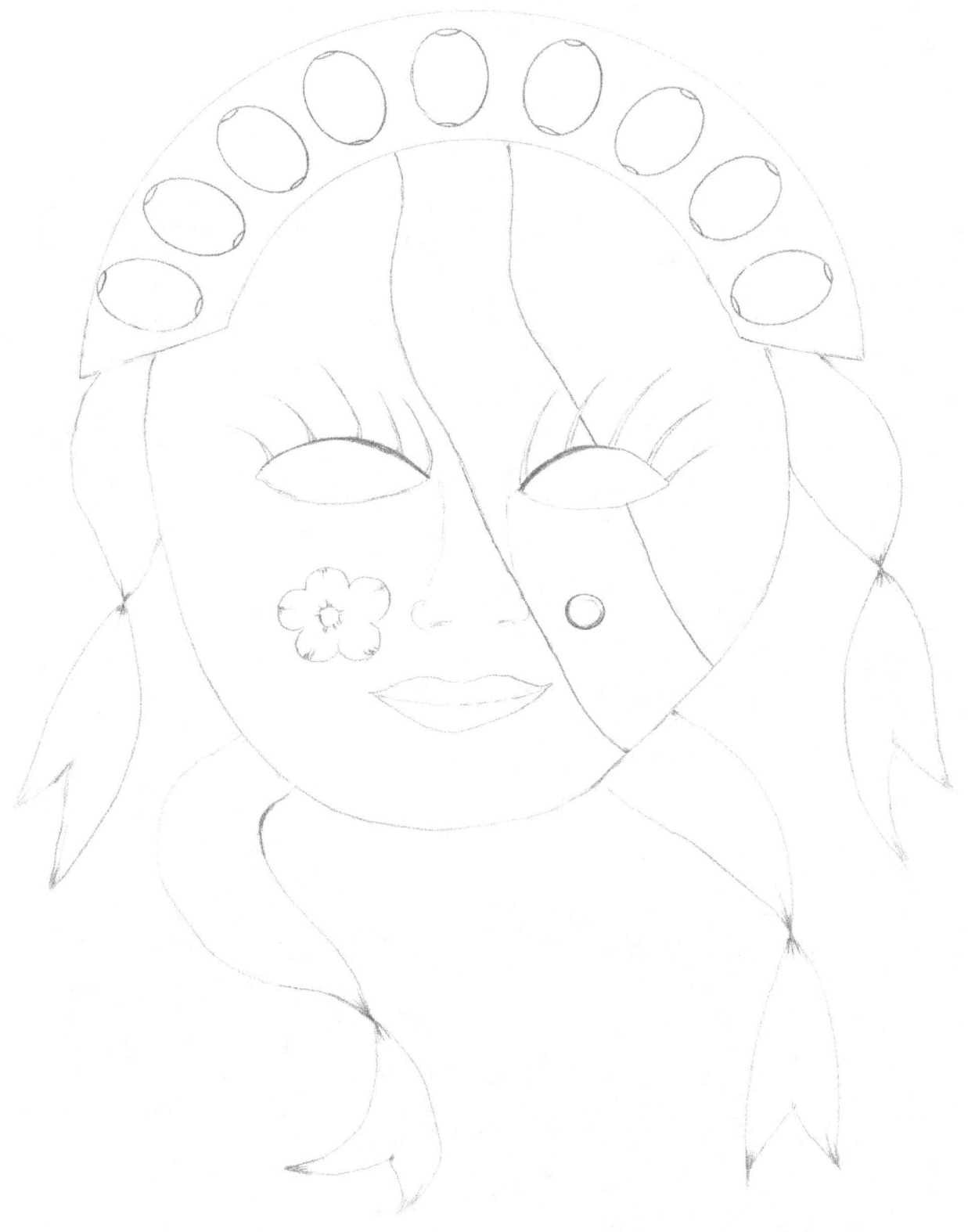

Carol Hopkins

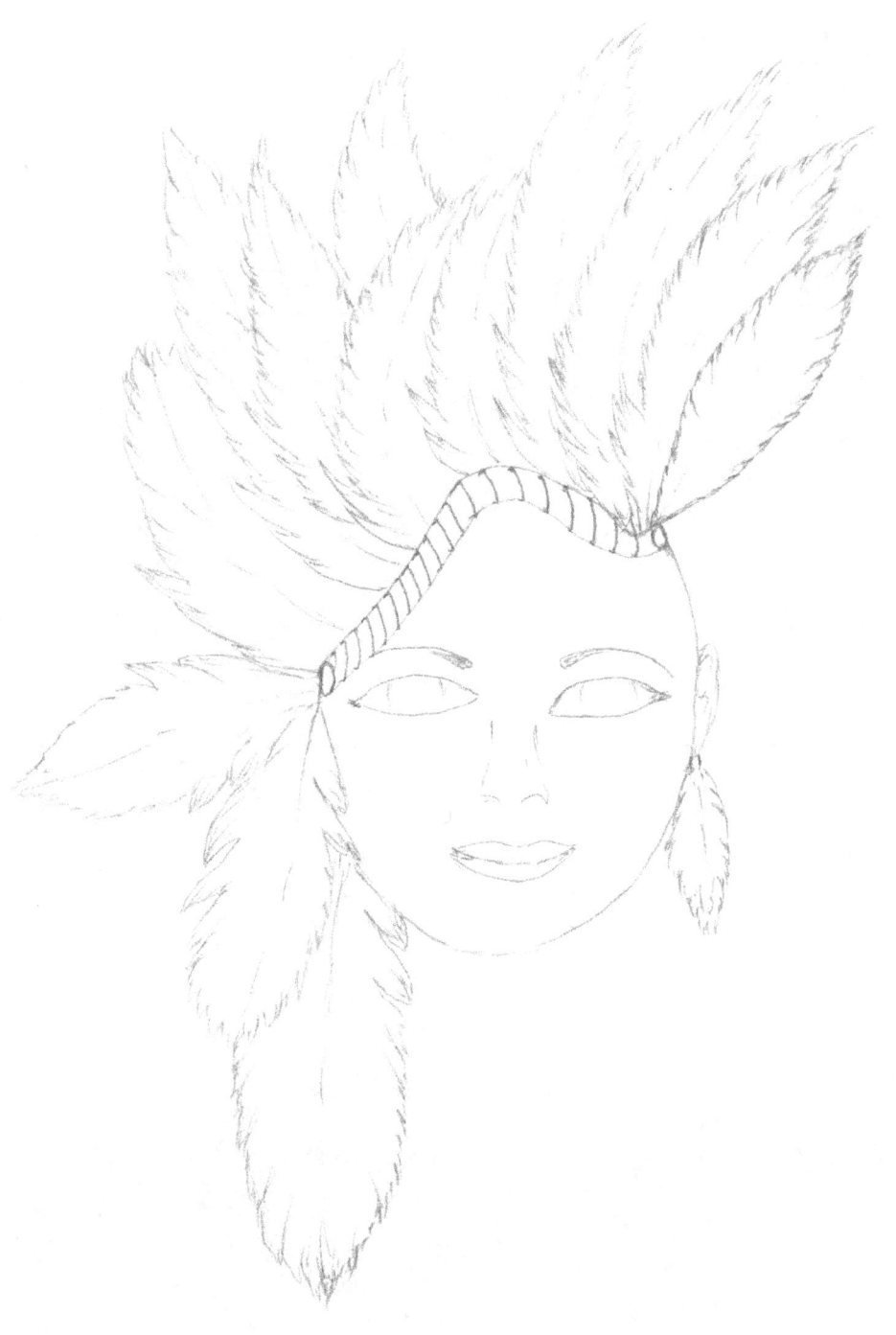

Carol Hopkins

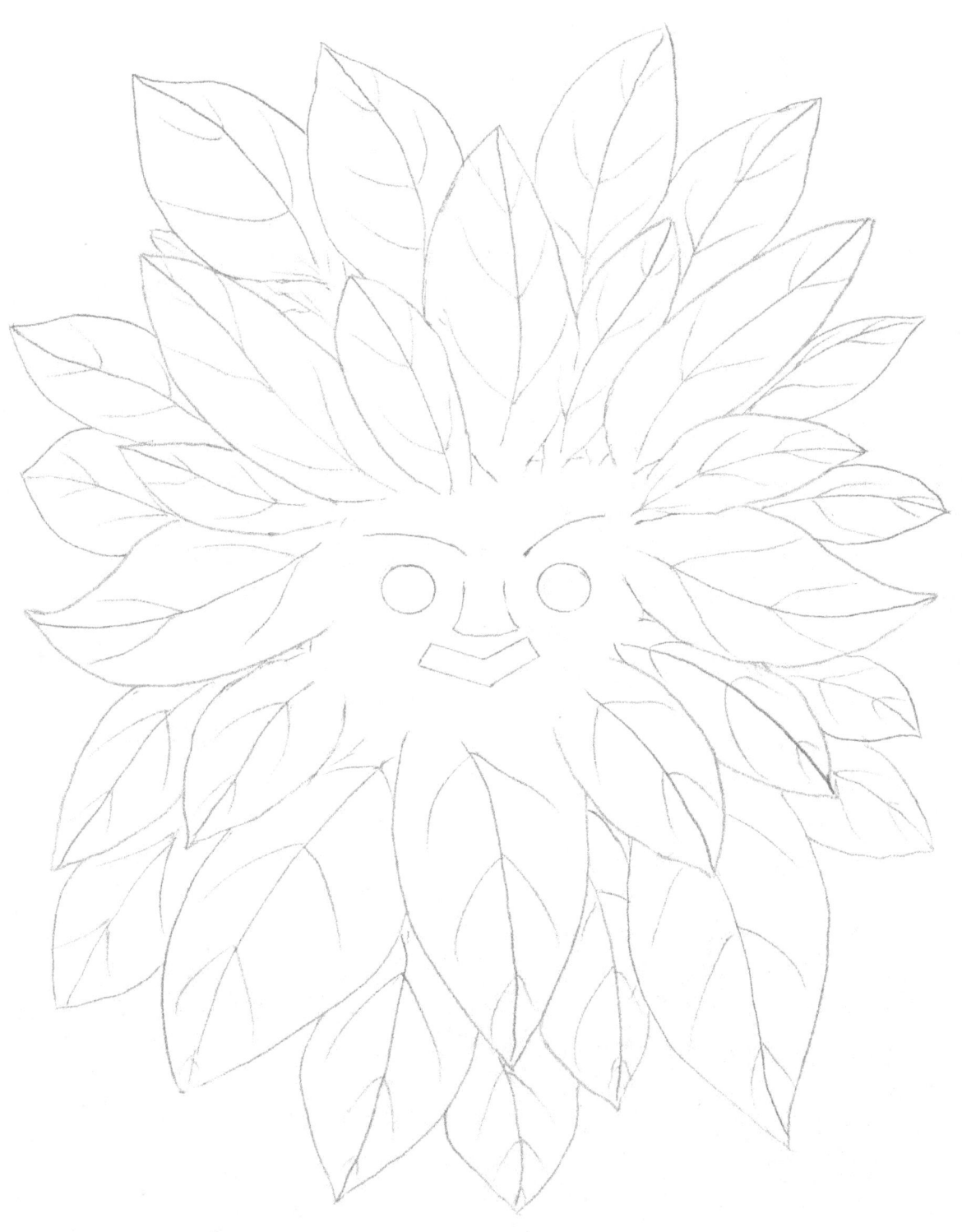

Carol Hopkins

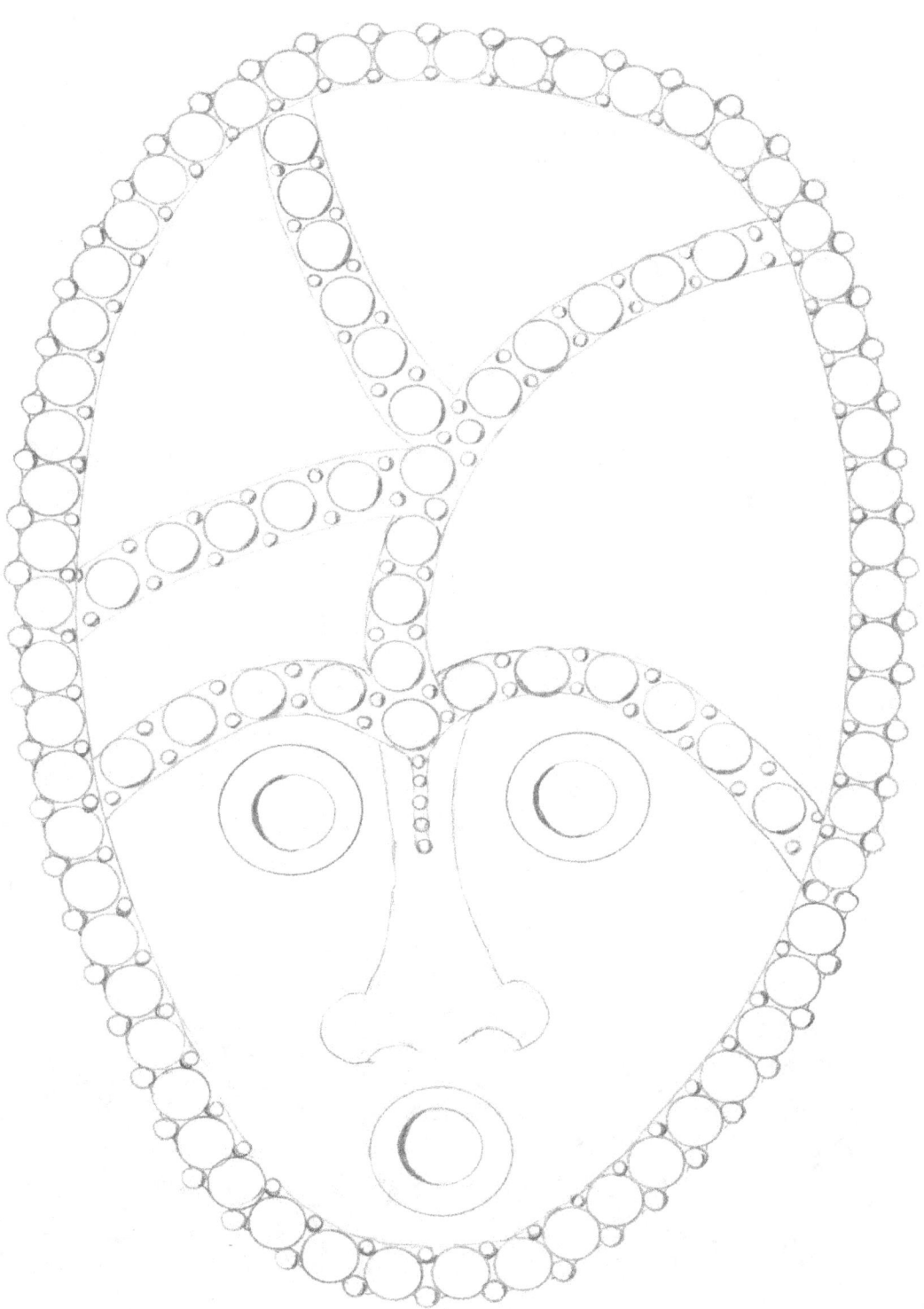

Carol Hopkins

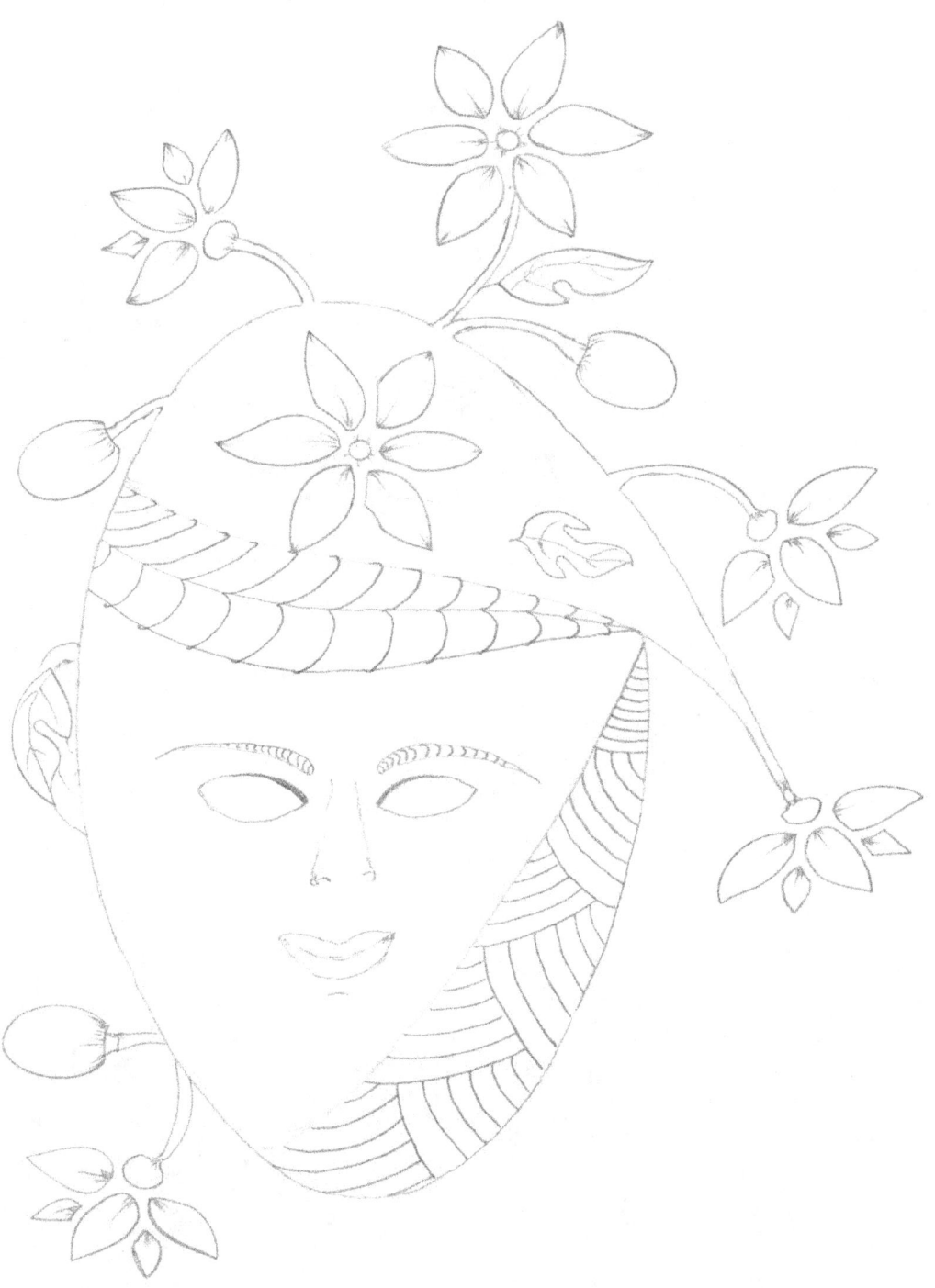

Carol Hopkins

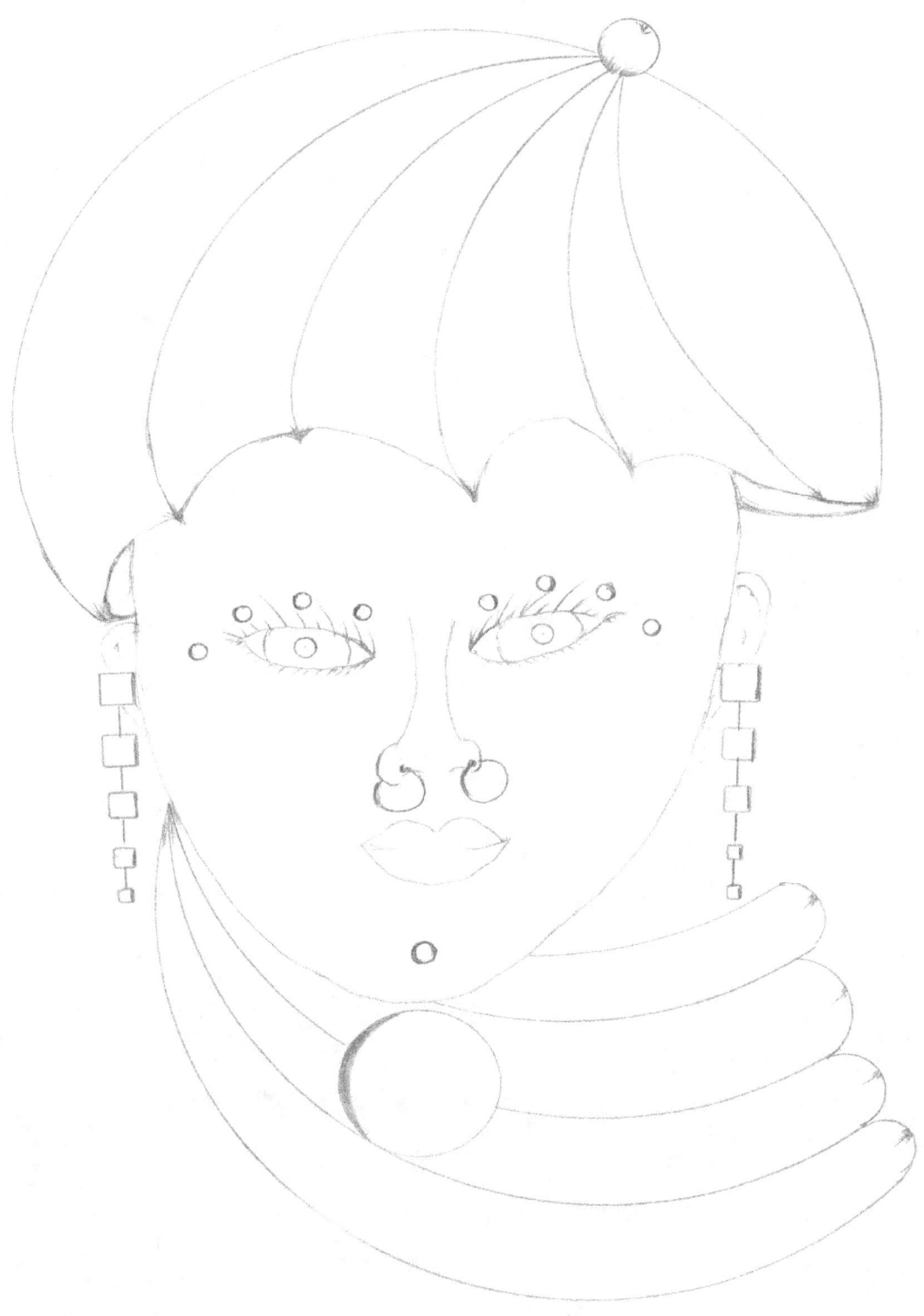

Carol Hopkins

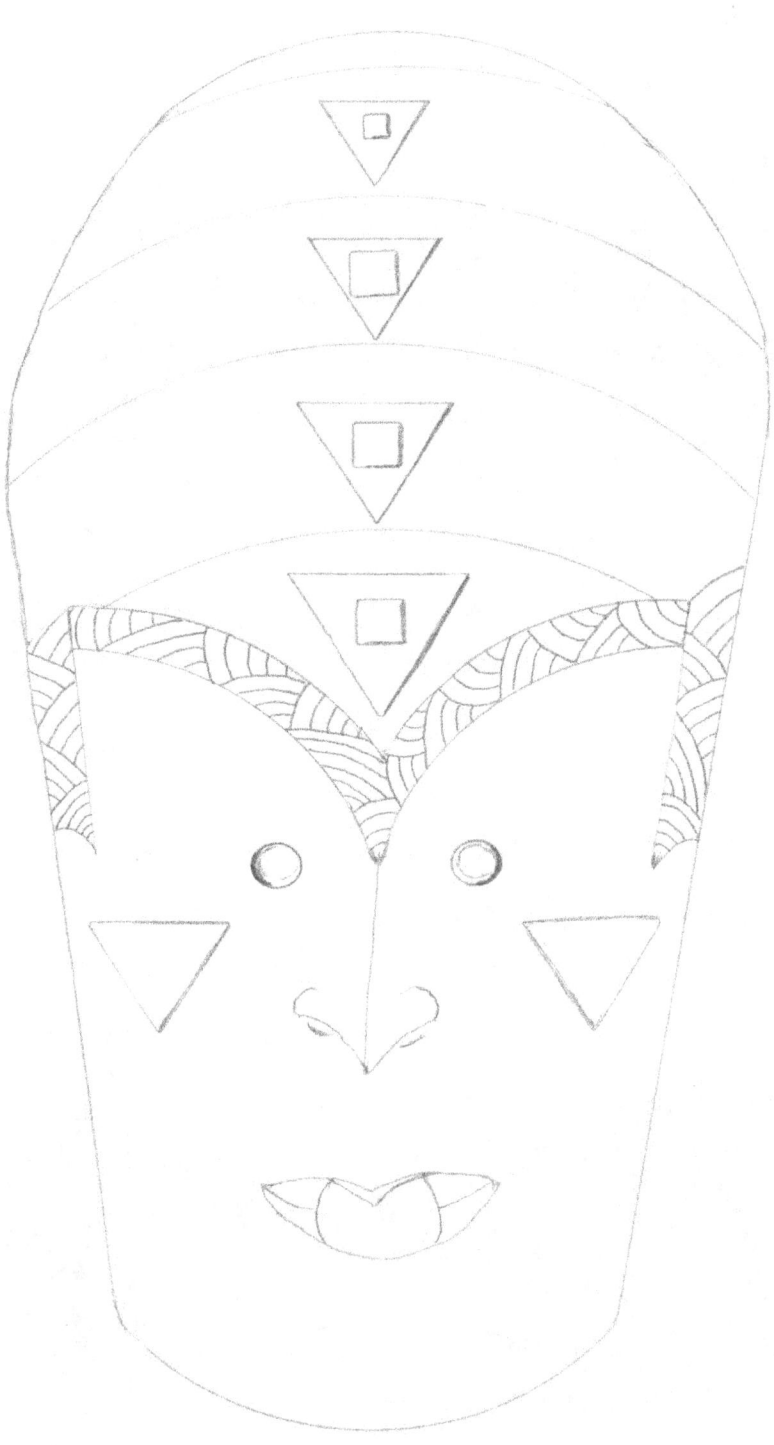

Carol Hopkins

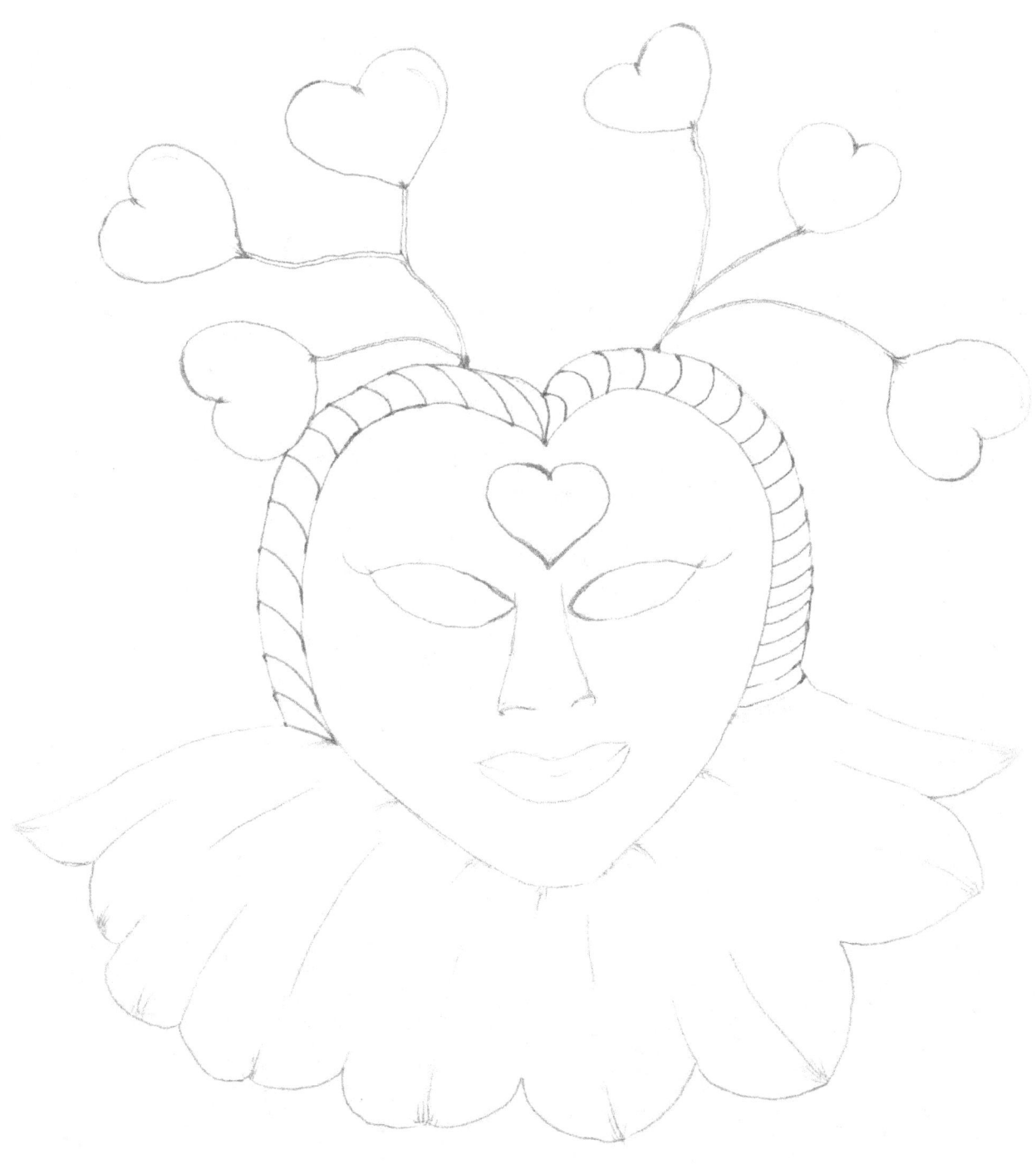

Carol Hopkins

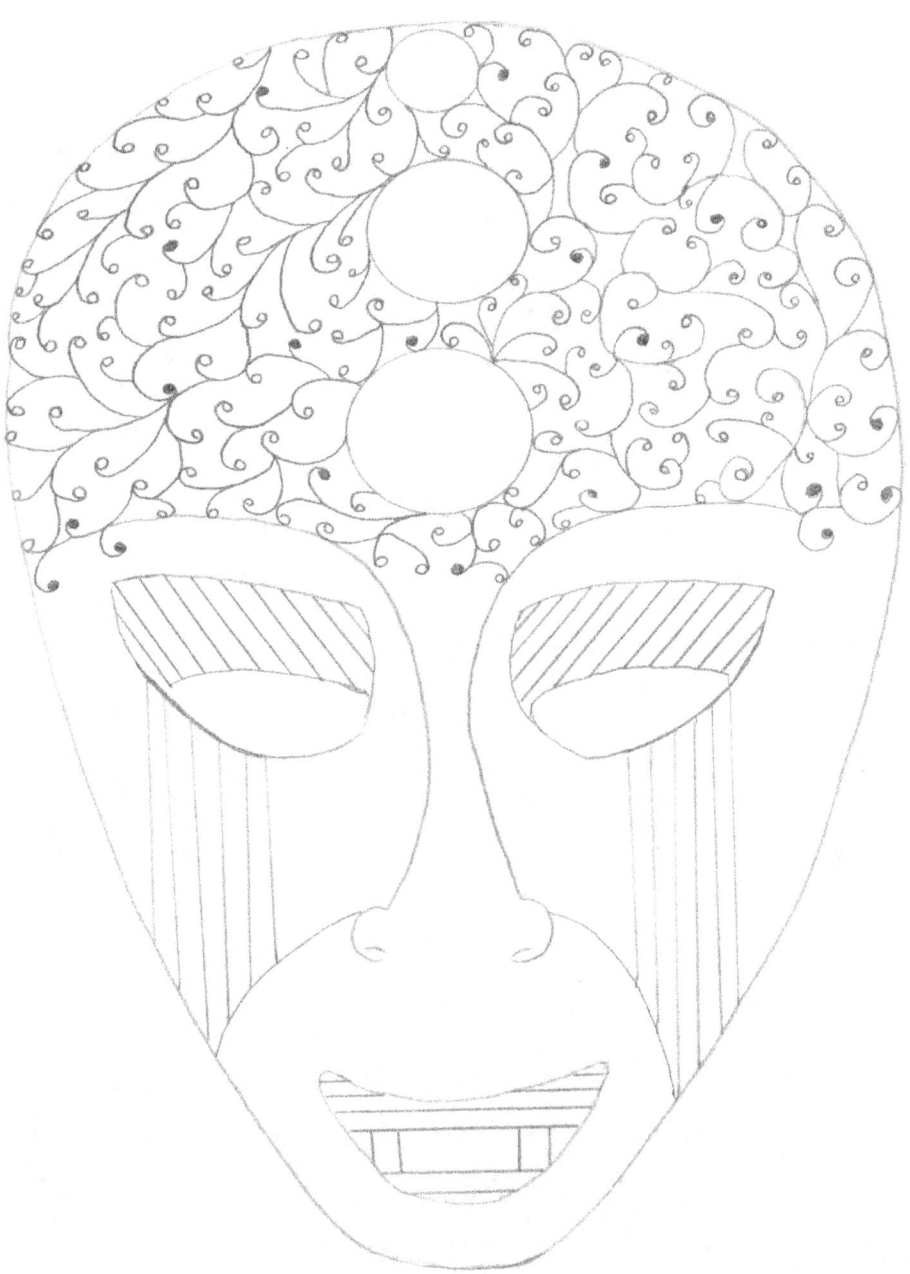

Carol Hopkins

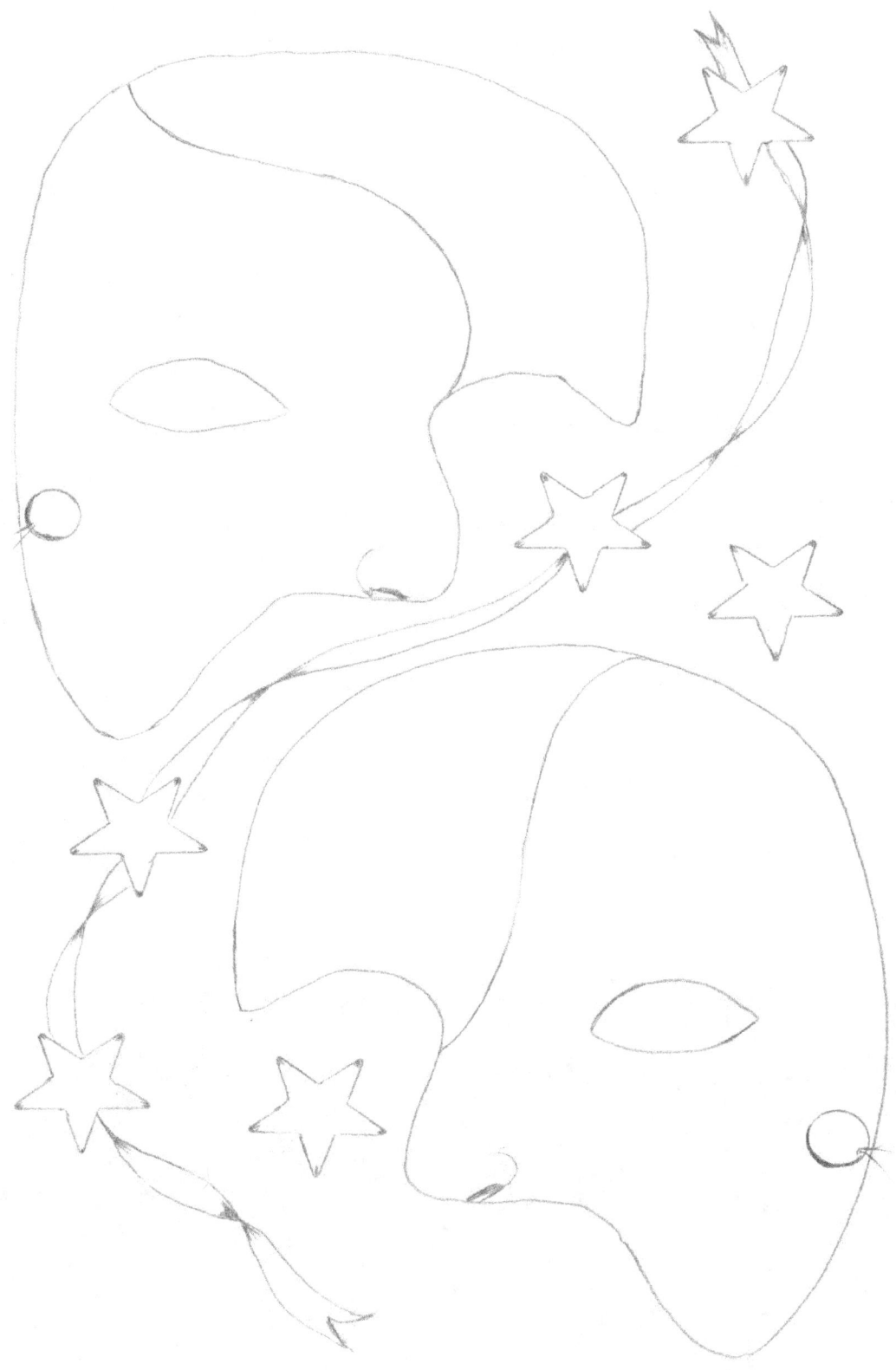

Carol Hopkins

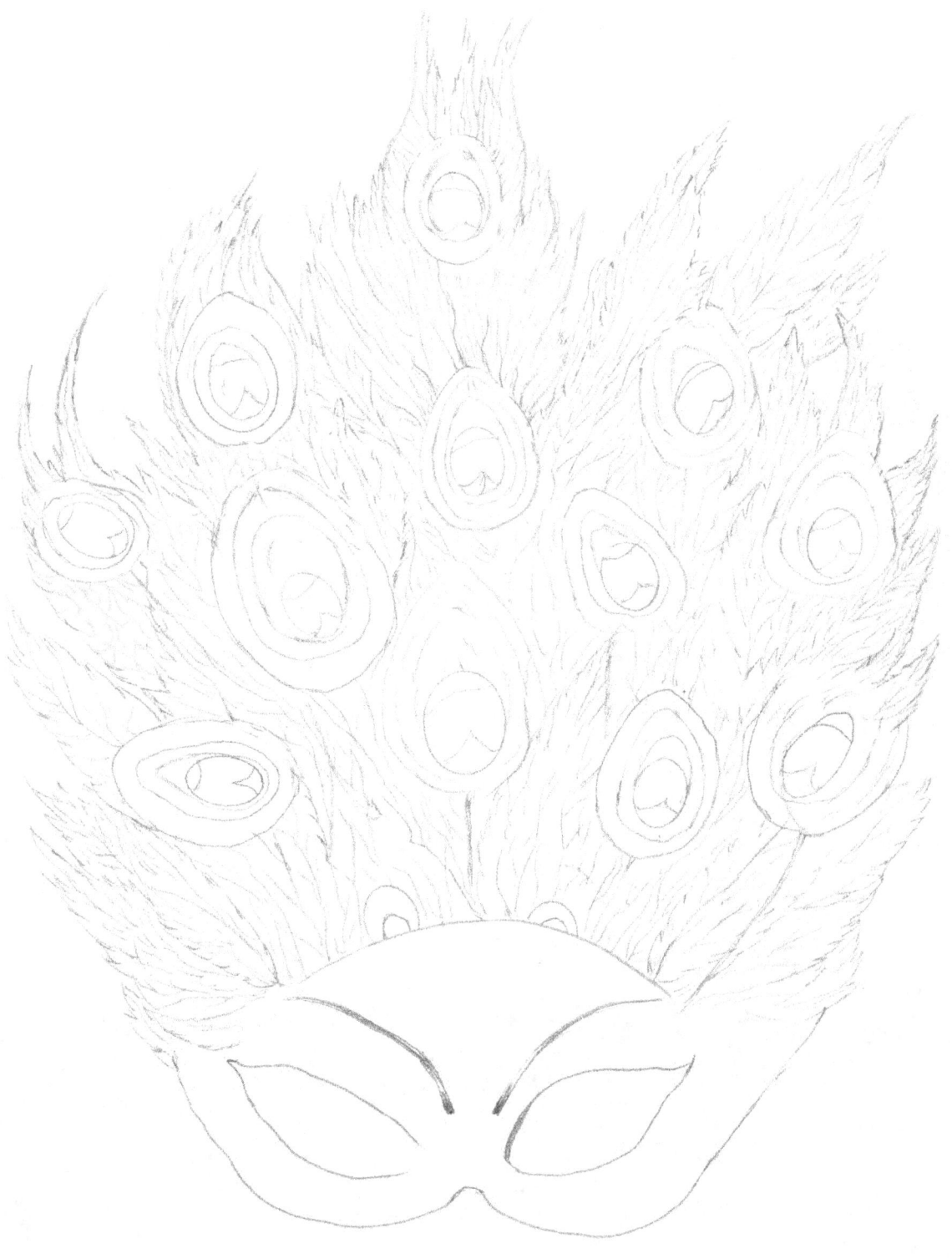

Carol Hopkins

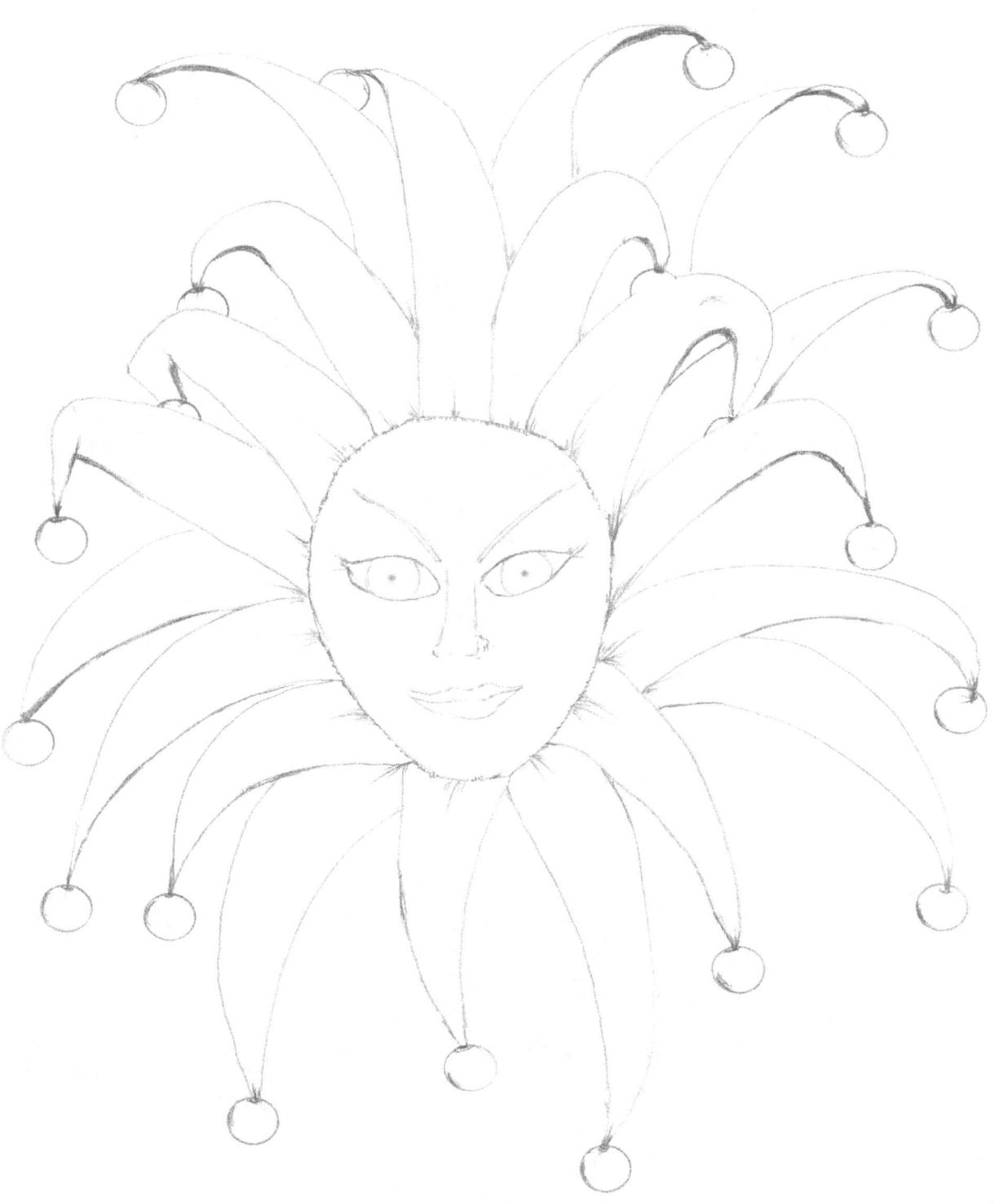

Carol Hopkins

Other Books Published by Carol Hopkins
"The Little Gardeners Series"

The Little Gardeners

Chester Learns to Fly

Butterflies

Together We Can Do It

Peep Goes Sailing

Hitching a Ride

Halloween

Thomas the Turkey

Christmas in the Garden

O Christmas Tree

Easter in the Garden

Up Up and Away

Veterans Day in the Garden

Uh-Oh We're Moving

Visit us: amazon.com/author/carolhopkins

Our Website: http://www.thelittlegardeners.com

Twitter Follow: @Whoispeep

FB. https://www.facebook.com/TheLittleGardeners/

www.ingramcontent.com/pod-product-compliance
Lightning Source LLC
Chambersburg PA
CBHW081557220526
45468CB00010B/2678